John Paul Jackson

אבת ו

315 Names of God

STREAMS
PUBLICATIONS

North Sutton, New Hampshire

I AM
365 Names of God
© 2002 by John Paul Jackson.

Requests for information should be addressed to:
Streams Publications
PO Box 550
North Sutton, NH 03260
http://www.streamsministries.com

Unless otherwise indicated, all Scripture quotations are taken from
The Holy Bible, New King James Version. © 1979, 1980, 1982 by
Thomas Nelson, Inc.

ISBN 1-58483-055-7

Printed on acid-free paper in the USA.

Dedication

✠

To my parents, Robert and Esther,
who first taught me all the treasures
hidden in the names of God, and
that God is still demonstrating the
inseparable nature of His acts,
His glory, and His names today.

To my wife, Diane, who by her life,
has taught me more about walking
with God than words can express.

Contents

Preface

Today in western culture, the power of a name has lost its significance. In a scriptural sense, a name isn't merely a label or a calling card. Rather, it encompasses the name as well as the reputation, fame, and glory an individual carries.

In the Bible, the word for "name" was used much more broadly, covering one's attributes, character traits, and even actions. David was not just a Psalmist-King's name. His name meant "beloved." Truly, David was beloved by God and man. It is difficult now to determine where his name, David, ended and where the idea of him being "beloved" began. His name and his character were intertwined so tightly.

This principle is espoused by Christian theologians. For example, *Strong's Concordance* and the *Dictionary of Biblical Imagery* suggests that the word "name" encompasses everything which the name covers, including the thoughts or feelings which are aroused by mentioning, hearing, and remembering the name. A name also highlights particular attributes of a person.

In this book, I have chosen to use God's names in their pure, biblical forms as terms used to describe the very essence, actions, and glory of God.

John Paul Jackson

Acknowledgments

✦

I am thankful to God for blessing us as we worked on this book. This book is a testament to the love, faith, and support of many people. I am indebted to those whose lives have surrounded mine and given substance to the ideas in this book. I am forever indebted to my wife, Diane, who gently shares the burden and joy of all my books.

I am especially grateful for the growing family at Streams Ministries whose generosity of spirit breathes passion, life, and joy into these pages. I am grateful to Jeannie Brooks for helping to organize my life so that I had time to write. To Greg Mapes and Mitch Brooks who help to create an atmosphere in which a project like this is possible, I express my deepest gratitude.

I want to thank Jordan Bateman, whose feel for poetry and rhythm has greatly enhanced the flow of this book. To Ed Tuttle who continues to astonish me with his creativity and who designed the beautiful pages in this book and contributed to the cover. To Jenny Bateman and Sarah Haig who helped with the research; to Don Archibald, Paul

Leary, Pat Leary, Roxanne Stewart, and Zach Mapes who assisted with proofreading. To Scott Cave for support in the early stage of the initial cover concept. To Carolyn Blunk, who oversaw the editing, design, and production of this book.

Finally, may the Holy Spirit enable each reader of this book to experience His presence and transforming power, to the glory of God.

✛

Introduction

✦

Weary from having traveled a long way, Jesus and the disciples were settling in for the night. As conversation began at dinnertime, Jesus listened keenly to His friends. Then He asked, "Who do people say I am?"

One answered, "Some say You are John the Baptist."

"Others say Elijah," said another.

"Some say Jeremiah or one of the prophets," replied a third.

Suddenly, as He had done many times over the months they had been together, Jesus turned the fireside chat on its ear. With eyes blazing with fire He asked them, "What about you? Who do you say I am?"

His question echoes prophetically throughout the ages. "Who do you say I am?" He asks each and every person who walks the earth.

Jesus knew the value and strength of God's name. When He taught His disciples to pray, He told them to "hallow" the Father's name. Meditate on the attributes, holiness, and purity of that name, He taught them. Treat that name with so much honor and affection that it becomes part of your lives. Jesus' call hasn't changed over the centuries. As His followers, we are still called to hallow His name.

To help us in that process, God has revealed many of His names and His character throughout the ages. Much is recorded in the Bible. In this book, I have collected more than 365 names and characteristics of God, and yet there were still more that I could have added. God's name is a rich tapestry of description, character, and holiness.

To enrich your devotional life, I have compiled 365 entries in this book, one for each day of the year. I listed these names into twelve categories: God of Wonders, God of Symbols, God of Mercy, God of Sacrifice, God of Justice, God of Promise, God the Shepherd, God the Ancient One, God the Reward, God the Warrior, God of Eternity, and God of Every Creature.

The Apostle Paul writes that Abraham's unwavering belief in God's character and purpose was "credited to him as righteousness," and that we, similarly, will be credited with righteousness if we believe in who He is (Romans 4). I encourage you to embrace God's names that are recorded in this book, and to know Him intimately, so that He might do the same for you.

God's names contain promises from God to His children. Knowing and believing His names will bring His blessing to your life in many areas:

Your health

Call on Jehovah Rapha, God who is healing, to care for you. There is no magic formula for healing, but absorbing God's name and calling on Him to bear witness to His name is a powerful faith-builder. I have read aloud these 365 names of God in several conferences and watched faith grow in the room, and listened as His presence is made manifest in the voices of those gathered. When we honor God's name, He will reveal His glory.

Your family

Many of us ache for God's blessing on our families. We have loved ones who have strayed from Him and we pray for them daily. God, too, is a Father whose heart longs for His children. In an instant, He can radically invade a life. As you read His names day after day, keep asking Him to reveal that characteristic to His wayward children. God's name is a promise to His faithful children: I AM your Father, and thus, all your household shall be saved (1 Corinthians 7:6).

Your friendships

As our friendship with God deepens, so does our friendship with others. It's a scriptural principle: We love because He first loved us. God, the One who sticks closer than a brother, shows us daily what it takes to be a true friend. By asking Him to brand us with His name and character, we begin to show that God-given beauty to those closest to us.

Your church

Jesus' bride should be the most radiantly beautiful part of God's creation. By corporately meditating on the names of God and asking Him to manifest the glory of those names in our churches, the majestic presence of God can be released corporately. It will take individual Christians who are unified in wholeheartedly seeking God's name to revitalize the Church.

Your provision

Jehovah Jireh, The Lord Will Provide, is a direct promise to God's children. God's provision is not just part of His mercy toward us, it is inherent in His character. The accumulation of God's names creates a momentum in the Spirit which releases divine provision. When hope and expectancy collide, it results in faith that releases miraculous provisions.

Why did God seed His names and attributes into Scripture? First, God wants to be known. He longs for us to be in relationship with Him. This was such a powerful desire that God sent His only begotten Son to earth to restore the ability for God and man to connect intimately (John 3:16).

Second, God wants us to reap the blessings that His names and attributes bring. God is the Creator and Designer of the universe. As such, He offers us divine protection and blessing, as long as we believe in the power that is inherent in His name. Time and again, the ancient Israelites saw divine protection that came with God's name. They knew that by calling on Jehovah God, He would save and deliver them, as well as release the awesome power contained in His name. Such a release often brought disaster upon their enemies. Even today, God's name is an open storehouse of blessing and a shield of protection for His children. His name is to be feared with the utmost reverence, and loved with the greatest affection.

However, simply knowing God's name is not enough. God longs for us to display His name in every circumstance. To love Him with such passion that we become like Him, that we carry and release the characteristics that His name implies into every situation.

As our loving heavenly Father, God is eager for us to realize that His names, His acts, and His glory are inseparable. His names describe His acts, and His acts release His glory. Thus, every act that He has performed throughout the ages serves as a reminder of God's rich character and fierce glory. They are one and the same. Furthermore, they are still available to us today.

In Revelation 22:4, we read that God's children will bear His name on their foreheads. But perhaps more importantly, as the prophet Isaiah said, they will bear the name of God in their hearts and in every fiber of their being. Therefore, as you meditate upon and call out to God, He will arise and place His name upon your life. He will chisel away at your character so that His name is beautifully displayed in your life. Bearing His name will take faith, testing, brokenness, obedience, submission, and work, but the rewards are immeasurable. We glorify God when we seek His names and attributes in our lives.

When He taught the disciples how to pray, Jesus said it was important to "hallow" (honor or revere as holy) God's name. As you ponder the names in this book, it is my prayer that you will discover a new reverence for God's marvelous name. As you read the entry on each page, I would like to encourage you to consider each one in these three ways:

Thought

Meditate on God's name. Ask Him to remind you of the times He has evidenced that name to you personally and to others. In the Bible, we are encouraged to ponder things that are true, noble, just, pure, lovely, things which are of a good report; we are admonished to meditate on virtuous and praiseworthy things. What could be purer, lovelier, nobler, truer, or more praiseworthy than the names and attributes of God?

Confession

When you read God's names, speak them aloud. It's important to verbally acknowledge the Lord's holiness. There is incredible power in speaking the name of God. The ancient Hebrews believed that every spoken word still vibrates in the atmosphere today.

Application

I would encourage you to develop a daily habit of reading and incorporating God's names in your life. As you practice the discipline of meditation on God's name, you will begin to walk in the blessing of God's name, and thereby, as Peter said, "become partakers of God's divine nature."

Reading and meditating on God's names kindles the fire of the Holy Spirit. Being praised for, and reminded of, His great name causes God to move. "Then those who feared the Lord spoke to one another, and the Lord listened and heard them," says Malachi 3:16. "So a book of remembrance was written before Him those who fear the Lord and who meditate on His name."

That book of remembrance was recorded in heavenly history. God loves to read it again and again. Every time you release the presence of God by calling on His name, God writes it down. That moment will be played over and over for His great joy. God remembers, listens, and savors your prayers.

It is important to learn God's names and understand the attributes they represent. Each day, take a page of this book and meditate and ponder what the Holy Spirit is saying. You may want to carry that name around with you all day, taking every opportunity possible to ponder God's name. You might put God's name on your wristwatch, and whenever you check the time, you will be reminded to think about God. After a few weeks, it will become natural to think of God in every instance.

Jesus' question resounds even now in our hearts: "Who do you say that I am?"

The Apostle Peter knew the answer instinctively that night near the fire. "You are the Christ, the Son of the Living God," he answered, full of conviction. Jesus gushed with emotion at Peter's confession of faith. "Blessed are you, Simon son of Jonah, for this was not revealed to you by man, but by My Father in heaven."

As you read this devotional, I pray that you, too, will be able to answer the Lord's question. May your love for God grow as you meditate on His names, attributes, and their beautiful characteristics. Ask God to make those features part of your life. Consider and worship God for His wondrous deeds. Truly, He is worthy of your praise. And remember God's whispered question: "Who do you say I am?"

Humans constantly change. Our soulish emotions fluctuate, our wills oscillate, and our flesh ages and weakens. That's why we need a marvelous God who can anchor us through the storms of life. ✦ God's wonders never change. His power and powerful acts are the same yesterday, today, and tomorrow. He is in control of the universe, showing His compassion and might in a myriad of ways. ✦ Meditate upon the wonders God has done in your life. What are the marvelous works which He has done during your friendship with Him? What secrets have you and He shared? What more does God have for you? What wonders will God show you in the coming weeks? What does God have in store for you in the days ahead?

God of Wonders

I AM

the God who shows wonders

✛

I will show wonders in heaven above
and signs in the earth beneath: blood
and fire and vapor of smoke.

Acts 2:19

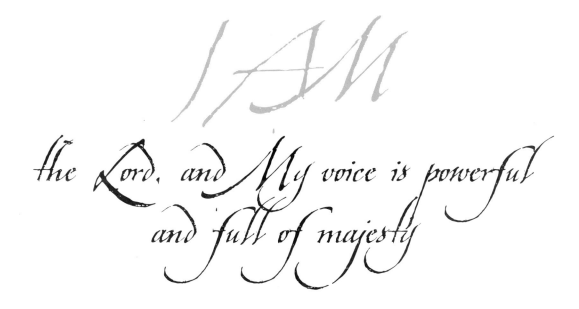

I AM the Lord, and My voice is powerful and full of majesty

✣

The voice of the Lord is powerful; the voice of the Lord is full of majesty.

Psalm 29:4

3

_I AM_

God; nothing is too hard for Me

✦

Behold, I am the Lord, the God of
all flesh. Is there anything
too hard for Me?

Jeremiah 32:27

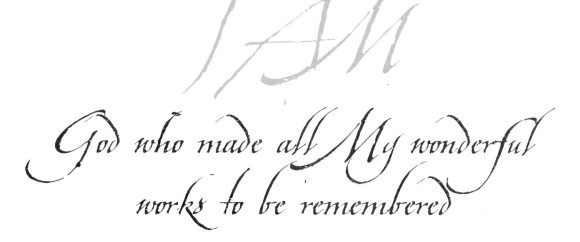

I AM God who made all My wonderful works to be remembered

✤

He has made His wonderful works to
be remembered; the Lord is gracious
and full of compassion.

Psalm 111:4

5

I AM

God and My glory thunders

✛

The voice of the Lord is over the
waters; the God of glory thunders; the
Lord is over many waters.

Psalm 29:3

I AM

the Spirit of knowledge and understanding

The Spirit of the Lord shall rest upon
Him, the Spirit of wisdom and
understanding, the Spirit of counsel
and might, the Spirit of knowledge
and of the fear of the Lord.

Isaiah 11:2

7

I AM

the Holy Spirit that moved upon the deep

❖

The earth was without form, and void;
and darkness was on the face of the
deep. And the Spirit of God was
hovering over the face of the waters.

Genesis 1:2

8

I AM

worthy of worship, glorious and incomparable

✦

Give to the Lord the glory due His
name; bring an offering, and come
before Him. Oh, worship the Lord in
the beauty of holiness!

1 Chronicles 16:29

9

I AM

God who makes Himself known through visions

✤

Then He said, 'If there is a prophet among you, I, the Lord, make Myself known to him in a vision; I speak to him in a dream.'

Numbers 12:6

I AM

dunamis power

✤

But you shall receive power [dunamis]
when the Holy Spirit has come upon
you; and you shall be witnesses to Me
in Jerusalem, and in all Judea and
Samaria, and to the end of the earth.

Acts 1:8

11

I AM

the giver of all revelation

✚

But God has revealed them to us
through His Spirit. For the Spirit
searches all things, yes, the deep
things of God.

1 Corinthians 2:10

I AM

glorious and full of weighty splendor

✛

If you do not carefully observe all the
words of this law that are written in
this book, that you may fear this
glorious and awesome name,
the Lord your God. . .

Deuteronomy 28:58

13

I AM

He that ascended to the Father

✤

Which He worked in Christ when
He raised Him from the dead and
seated Him at His right hand
in the heavenly places. . .

Ephesians 1:20

14

I AM

the Triune God of Israel

✚

But the Helper, the Holy Spirit,
whom the Father will send in My
name, He will teach you all things,
and bring to your remembrance all
things that I said to you.

John 14:26

I AM

God who performs signs

✦

. . .and that you may tell in the
hearing of your son and your son's
son the mighty things I have done in
Egypt, and My signs which I have done
among them, that you may know that
I am the Lord.

Exodus 10:2

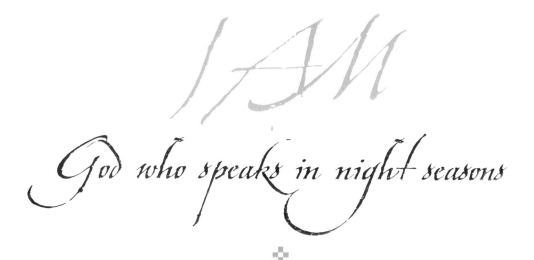

I AM

God who speaks in night seasons

✠

...If there is a prophet among you,

I, the Lord, make Myself known

to him in a vision;

I speak to him in a dream.

Numbers 12:6

17

I AM

the King of glory

✠

Who is this King of glory?
The Lord strong and mighty,
the Lord mighty in battle.

Psalm 24:8

I AM

He who searches the mind and heart

✠

...all the churches shall know that I
am He who searches the minds and
hearts. And I will give to each one of
you according to your works.

Revelation 2:23

19

I AM

great and greatly to be praised

✤

For the Lord is great and greatly
to be praised; He is also to be
feared above all gods.

1 Chronicles 16:25

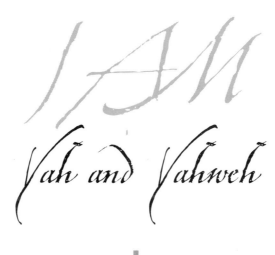

I AM

Yah and Yahweh

✦

Sing to God, sing praises to His name;
extol Him who rides on the clouds, by
His name Yah, and rejoice before Him.

Psalm 68:4

I AM

the Creator of all true worship

✦

God is Spirit, and those who worship
Him must worship in spirit and truth.

John 4:24

22

wisdom

✤

Counsel is mine, and sound wisdom;
I am understanding, I have strength.
I love those who love me, and those
who seek me diligently will find me.

Proverbs 8:14 and 17

23

I AM

omniscient

✚

Because the foolishness of God is
wiser than men, and the weakness of
God is stronger than men.

1 Corinthians 1:25

24

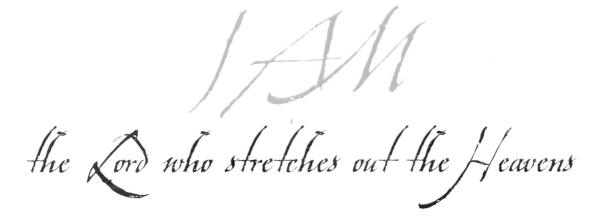

I AM

the Lord who stretches out the Heavens

✦

Thus says the Lord, your Redeemer,
and He who formed you from the
womb: 'I am the Lord, who makes all
things, who stretches out the heavens
all alone, who spreads abroad the
earth by Myself.'

Isaiah 44:24

I AM

God who speaks

✦

Therefore My people shall know My
name; therefore they shall know in
that day that I am He who speaks:
'Behold, it is I.'

Isaiah 52:6

26

I AM

Jehovah–Rapha, your healer

There He made a statute and an ordinance for them, and there He tested them, and said, 'If you diligently heed the voice of the Lord your God and do what is right in His sight, give ear to His commandments and keep all His statutes, I will put none of the diseases on you which I have brought on the Egyptians. For I am the Lord who heals you.'

Exodus 15:25b-26

I AM

God who declares new things before they spring forth

✚

Behold, the former things have
come to pass, and new things I
declare; before they spring forth
I tell you of them.

Isaiah 42:9

28

_I AM_

the answer of your tongue

✜

The preparations of the heart
belong to man, but the answer of
the tongue is from the Lord.

Proverbs 16:1

29

I AM

prophecy fulfilled: never early, never late

✛

Then He said to them, 'These are the
words which I spoke to you while I was
still with you, that all things must be
fulfilled which were written in the Law
of Moses and the Prophets and the
Psalms concerning Me.'

Luke 24:44

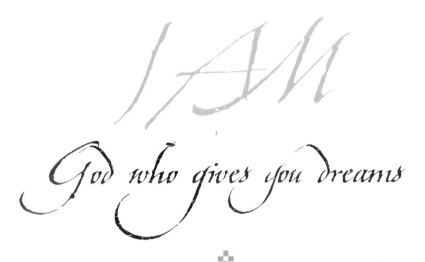

I AM

God who gives you dreams

✣

And it shall come to pass in the last
days, says God, that I will pour out of
My Spirit on all flesh; your sons and
your daughters shall prophesy, your
young men shall see visions, your old
men shall dream dreams.

Acts 2:17

I AM
above all who are thought to be gods

✦

Now I know that the Lord is greater
than all the gods; for in the very thing
in which they behaved proudly,
He was above them.

Exodus 18:11

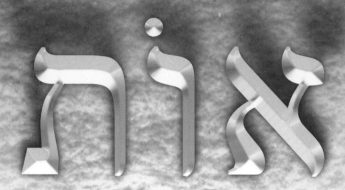

The Bible is full of symbolic language, down-to-earth, practical illustrations of deep spiritual truth. As we ponder the mysteries of God, biblical metaphors give us much-needed direction and focus. Take the rainbow. First given thousands of years ago as a promise to Noah, God ordained the power of that symbol. ✤ Jesus used parables throughout His earthly ministry to reveal spiritual truths. Perhaps there is no deeper, more powerful symbol than the bread and wine of communion; the consumption of Christ's sacrifice, the remembrance of the Cross, the feast the Kingdom of God was built on. ✤ Search the symbols listed in this section for the deep things of God. What does God illustrate in His chosen metaphors? What truth lies beneath the surface? What does God have for you today?

God of Symbols

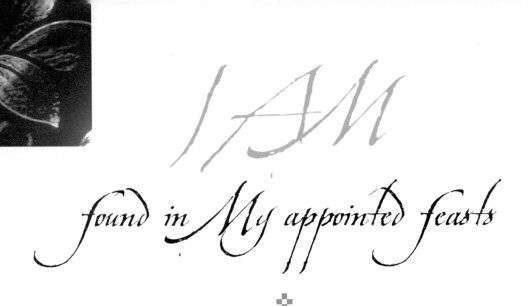

I AM

found in My appointed feasts

✦

Also in the day of your gladness, in your
appointed feasts, and at the beginning of
your months, you shall blow the trumpets
over your burnt offerings and over the
sacrifices of your peace offerings; and they
shall be a memorial for you before your God:
I am the Lord your God.

Numbers 10:10

I AM

the anointing oil

✣

. . .nor shall he go out of the
sanctuary, nor profane the sanctuary
of his God; for the consecration
of the anointing oil of his God is
upon him: I am the Lord.

Leviticus 21:12

I AM
the bright cloud that comes to you

✛

While he was still speaking, behold,
a bright cloud overshadowed them;
and suddenly a voice came out of the
cloud, saying, 'This is My beloved
Son, in whom I am well pleased.
Hear Him!'

Matthew 17:5

38

I AM

the synagogue, church, tabernacle, and temple

✛

You shall keep My Sabbaths
and reverence My sanctuary:
I am the Lord.

Leviticus 19:30

I AM

the living water of life

✜

But whoever drinks of the water that I
shall give him will never thirst. But the
water that I shall give him will become
in him a fountain of water springing
up into everlasting life.

John 4:14

I AM

the shofar trumpet

✢

Then it came to pass on the third day,
in the morning, that there were
thunderings and lightnings, and a
thick cloud on the mountain; and the
sound of the trumpet [shofar] was very
loud, so that all the people who were
in the camp trembled.

Exodus 19:16

I AM

the fountain of Israel

✚

Bless God in the congregations, the
Lord, from the fountain of Israel.

Psalm 68:26

I AM

Israel's living star

✦

I see Him, but not now; I behold Him,
but not near; a star shall come out of
Jacob; a scepter shall rise out of Israel,
and batter the brow of Moab, and
destroy all the sons of tumult.

Numbers 24:17

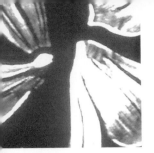

I AM

the Passover

❖

Therefore purge out the old leaven,

that you may be a new lump, since

you truly are unleavened.

For indeed Christ, our Passover,

was sacrificed for us.

1 Corinthians 5:7

I AM
the Ark of the Covenant

✤

Arise, O Lord, to Your resting place,
You and the ark of Your strength.

Psalm 132:8

45

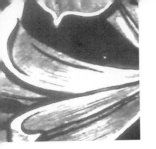

I AM
the Door

✠

I am the door. If anyone enters by Me,
he will be saved, and will go in and
out and find pasture.

John 10:9

I AM

the altar of the tabernacle

✤

We have an altar from which
those who serve the tabernacle
have no right to eat.

Hebrews 13:10

47

I AM
the balm of Gilead

✤

. . . Is there no balm in Gilead,

is there no physician there?

Jeremiah 8:22

I AM

the rose of Sharon

✤

I am the rose of Sharon,

and the lily of the valleys.

Song of Solomon 2:1

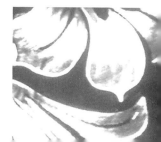

I AM

the tree of life

✢

He who has an ear, let him hear what
the Spirit says to the churches. To him
who overcomes I will give to eat from
the tree of life, which is in the midst
of the Paradise of God.

Revelation 2:7

I AM

the God of Bethel

✛

Then Jacob awoke from his sleep and
said, 'Surely the Lord is in this place,
and I did not know it.' And he called
the name of that place Bethel.

Genesis 28:16 and 19

51

I AM

the lily of the valley

✤

I am the rose of Sharon,

and the lily of the valleys.

Song of Solomon 2:1

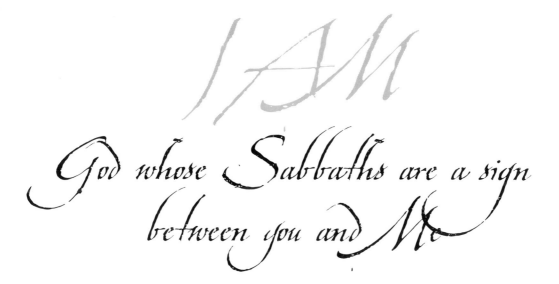

I AM

God whose Sabbaths are a sign between you and Me

✛

Moreover I also gave them My
Sabbaths, to be a sign between them
and Me, that they might know that I
am the Lord who sanctifies them.

Ezekiel 20:12

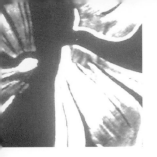

I AM

the rainbow's color

❖

I set My rainbow in the cloud, and it
shall be for the sign of the covenant
between Me and the earth.

Genesis 9:13

I AM

the Rock, there is no other

✛

Do not fear, nor be afraid; have I not
told you from that time, and declared
it? You are My witnesses. Is there a
God besides Me? Indeed there is no
other Rock; I know not one.

Isaiah 44:8

55

I AM
the glory in the cloud of the temple

✤

Then the glory of the Lord went up
from the cherub, and paused over the
threshold of the temple; and the house
was filled with the cloud, and the
court was full of the brightness
of the Lord's glory.

Ezekiel 10:4

I AM
the bread of life

✛

And Jesus said to them, 'I am the bread of life. He who comes to Me shall never hunger, and he who believes in Me shall never thirst.'

John 6:35

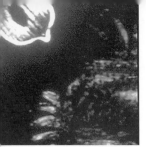

I AM

your Rock, full of living water

✦

. . .and all drank the same spiritual

drink. For they drank of that

spiritual Rock that followed them,

and that Rock was Christ.

1 Corinthians 10:4

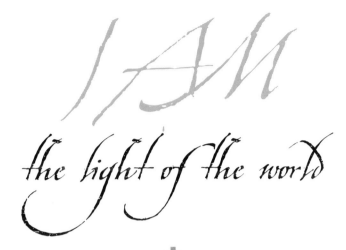

I AM

the light of the world

❖

As long as I am in the world,

I am the light of the world.

John 9:5

I AM

a consuming fire

✠

For the Lord your God is a
consuming fire, a jealous God.

Deuteronomy 4:24

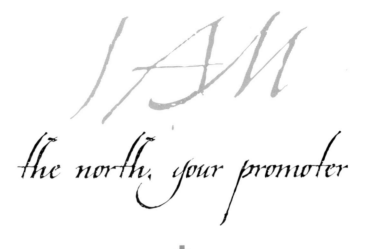

I AM

the north, your promoter

✛

For exaltation comes neither from the
east nor from the west nor from the
south. But God is the Judge: He puts
down one, and exalts another.

Psalm 75:6-7

61

I AM
the Bright and Morning Star

✦

I, Jesus, have sent My angel to testify
to you these things in the churches. I
am the Root and the Offspring of
David, the Bright and Morning Star.

Revelation 22:16

I AM

the light—luminous, glowing,
and radiant One

✦

This is the message which we have
heard from Him and declare to you,
that God is light and in Him is
no darkness at all.

1 John 1:5

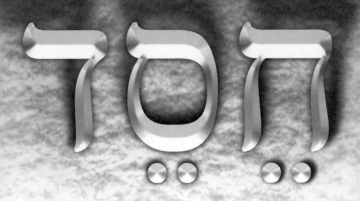

God of Mercy

God's mercy is one of the most powerful themes running through the Bible. Imagine a perfect, omnipresent, all-powerful God showing mercy by feeding manna to the Israelites wandering in the desert. Or, strengthening Gideon through a dream that foretold his enemy's defeat. Or, forgiving King David who had committed adultery and murder. Or, using ravens to feed Elijah. Or, providing for widows, orphans, and refugees. Scripture is a powerful testimony to God's mercy. ✢ Perhaps the greatest example of God's merciful nature is His ability and desire to forgive our sin. Mercy is not getting what you deserve; rather, it's getting what you don't deserve. It's God's kindness demonstrated toward you. ✢ Over the years, God has extended incredible mercy to you. God loves you more than you can even imagine. Every morning, He wants to shower you with new mercies. Today, ask God to continue to pour out mercy on you and your family.

I AM

God who is merciful

✛

Go and proclaim these words toward
the north, and say: 'Return,
backsliding Israel,' says the Lord; 'I
will not cause My anger to fall on you.
For I am merciful,' says the Lord; 'I
will not remain angry forever.'

Jeremiah 3:12

66

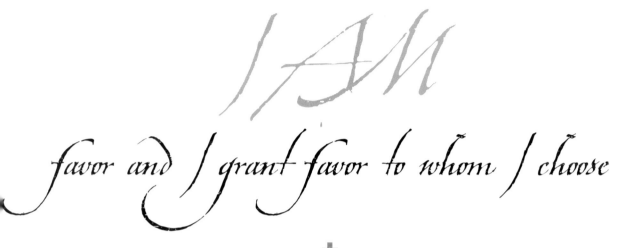

I AM favor and I grant favor to whom I choose

✤

And the Lord had given the people
favor in the sight of the Egyptians,
so that they granted them what
they requested. Thus they
plundered the Egyptians.

Exodus 12:36

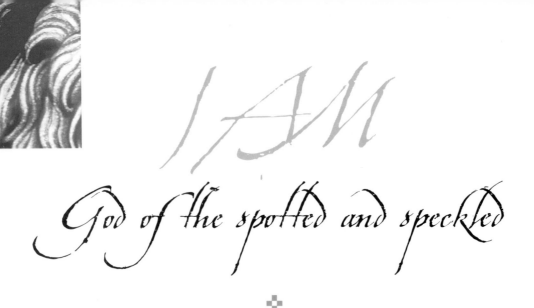

I AM

God of the spotted and speckled

✛

Then the Angel of God spoke to me in
a dream, saying, 'Jacob.' And I said,
'Here I am.' And He said, 'Lift your
eyes now and see, all the rams which
leap on the flocks are streaked,
speckled, and gray-spotted; for I have
seen all that Laban is doing to you.'

Genesis 31:11-12

I AM

the Prince of Peace, prophesied by the prophet Isaiah

✦

For unto us a Child is born, unto us a Son is
given; and the government will be upon His
shoulder. And His name will be called
Wonderful, Counselor, Mighty God,
Everlasting Father, Prince of Peace.

Isaiah 9:6

I AM

God who restores your soul

✠

He restores my soul; He leads me in
the paths of righteousness for His
name's sake.

Psalm 23:3

I AM

the friend of sinners

✠

The Son of Man came eating and
drinking, and they say, 'Look, a
glutton and a winebibber, a friend of
tax collectors and sinners!' But
wisdom is justified by her children.

Matthew 11:19

I AM

God, I tempt no one

✦

No temptation has overtaken you except
such as is common to man; but God is
faithful, who will not allow you to be
tempted beyond what you are able, but
with the temptation will also make the way
of escape, that you may be able to bear it.

1 Corinthians 10:13

I AM

the God of peace

✣

Now may the God of peace who
brought up our Lord Jesus from the
dead, that great Shepherd of the
sheep, through the blood of the
everlasting covenant. . .

Hebrews 13:20

73

I AM

He who weeps with those who weep

✤

Rejoice with those who rejoice, and

weep with those who weep.

Romans 12:15

I AM

He who speaks from a position of mercy

✛

Now when Moses went into the tabernacle
of meeting to speak with Him, he heard
the voice of One speaking to him from
above the mercy seat that was on the ark
of the Testimony, from between the two
cherubim; thus He spoke to him.

Numbers 7:89

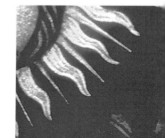

I AM

longsuffering

✦

The Lord is longsuffering and
abundant in mercy, forgiving iniquity
and transgression.

Numbers 14:18a

I AM
My Spirit

✦

Now the Lord is the Spirit; and
where the Spirit of the Lord is,
there is liberty.

2 Corinthians 3:17

I AM

gracious

✤

For that is his only covering, it is
his garment for his skin. What will
he sleep in? And it will be that
when he cries to Me, I will hear,
for I am gracious.

Exodus 22:27

I AM

the forgiver of all transgressions

✠

Have mercy upon me, O God, according
to Your lovingkindness; according to the
multitudes of Your tender mercies, blot
out my transgressions.

Psalm 51:1

I AM

the manna which came down from Heaven

✜

The Jews then complained about Him,
because He said, 'I am the bread
which came down from heaven.'

John 6:41

I AM

the breath that gives you life

✦

The Spirit of God has made me,

and the breath of the Almighty

gives me life.

Job 33:4

81

I AM
He who will not remember your sins

✦

I, even I, am He who blots out your
transgressions for My own sake; and I
will not remember your sins.

Isaiah 43:25

I AM

the beloved in the Song of songs

❖

He brought me to the
banqueting house, and his
banner over me was love.

Song of Solomon 2:4

83

I AM

God who stretches out His hand

✛

And the Egyptians shall know that I
am the Lord, when I stretch out My
hand on Egypt and bring out the
children of Israel from among them.

Exodus 7:5

I AM

the liberty you seek through my Spirit

✠

Now the Lord is the Spirit; and
where the Spirit of the Lord is,
there is liberty.

2 Corinthians 3:17

I AM

ever faithful

✠

Now I saw heaven opened, and
behold, a white horse. And He who
sat on him was called Faithful
and True, and in righteousness
He judges and makes war.

Revelation 19:11

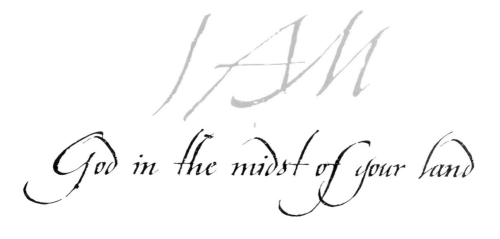

I AM

God in the midst of your land

✠

And in that day I will set apart the
land of Goshen, in which My people
dwell, that no swarms of flies shall be
there, in order that you may know that
I am the Lord in the midst of the land.

Exodus 8:22

87

I AM

the forgiver of iniquity

✛

Bless the Lord, O my soul, and forget not
all His benefits: who forgives all your
iniquities, who heals all your diseases.

Psalm 103:2-3

I AM

abundant in mercy

✛

The Lord is longsuffering and
abundant in mercy, forgiving iniquity
and transgression.

Numbers 14:18a

I AM
the altar of peace for your fear

✤

So Gideon built an altar there
to the Lord, and called it
The-Lord-Is-Peace. To this day it
is still in Ophrah of the Abiezrites.

Judges 6:24

I AM

the Lord who makes wise the simple

✦

The law of the Lord is perfect,
converting the soul; the testimony
of the Lord is sure, making
wise the simple.

Psalm 19:7

I AM

God who is daily full of new mercy

✠

Through the Lord's mercies we are not
consumed, because His compassions
fail not. They are new every morning;
great is Your faithfulness.

Lamentations 3:22-23

I AM
God who comforts you

✜

I, even I, am He who comforts you.
Who are you that you should be afraid
of a man who will die, and of the son
of a man who will be made like grass?

Isaiah 51:12

I AM

God of the poor and stranger

✣

When you reap the harvest of your land,
you shall not wholly reap the corners of
your field when you reap, nor shall you
gather any gleaning from your harvest.
You shall leave them for the poor and for
the stranger: I am the Lord your God.

Leviticus 23:22

I AM

gentle and lowly in heart

✢

Take My yoke upon you and learn
from Me, for I am gentle and lowly
in heart, and you will find
rest for your souls.

Matthew 11:29

95

I AM

the Lord who exercises lovingkindness

✜

'But let him who glories glory in this,

that he understands and knows Me,

that I am the Lord, exercising

lovingkindness, judgment, and

righteousness in the earth. For in

these I delight,' says the Lord.

Jeremiah 9:24

God offered a sacrifice by sending His only begotten Son to earth. Imagine how painful it was for our Heavenly Father to watch His Son be ridiculed and wrongfully accused. Consider how difficult it was for God to allow His own creation to kill His Son. One can only imagine the agony the Father suffered in watching Jesus breathe His last breath. But His sacrifice was a step in the journey of reconciling mankind with God, a wonderful gift Jesus Christ gave the world. ✣ Meditate on that holy sacrifice and what it has done for you. ✣ In our daily lives, obedience is often better than sacrifice. Sometimes the most difficult thing to do is to obey God, because it means giving up our agenda for that moment. That's how our obedience becomes a sacrifice.

God of Sacrifice

I AM

the Christ

✦

He said to them, 'But who do you say
that I am?' Peter answered and said,
'The Christ of God.'

Luke 9:20

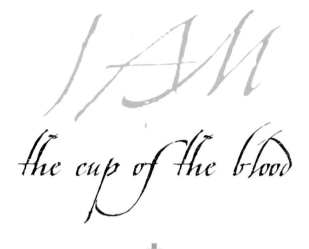

I AM
the cup of the blood

✦

Likewise He also took the cup after
supper, saying, 'This cup is the
new covenant in My blood,
which is shed for you.'

Luke 22:20

I AM

the eternal sacrifice

✠

But this Man, after He had offered one
sacrifice for sins forever, sat down at the
right hand of God, from that time waiting
till His enemies are made His footstool.
For by one offering He has perfected
forever those who are being sanctified.

Hebrews 10:12-14

I AM
the blood that cleanses you from sin

✦

But if we walk in the light as He is in
the light, we have fellowship with one
another, and the blood of Jesus Christ
His Son cleanses us from all sin.

1 John 1:7

103

I AM

the crucified Messiah of Calvary

✠

Therefore let all the house of Israel
know assuredly that God has made
this Jesus, whom you crucified,
both Lord and Christ.

Acts 2:36

I AM

your righteousness

✛

Clouds and darkness surround Him;
righteousness and justice are the
foundation of His throne.

Psalm 97:2

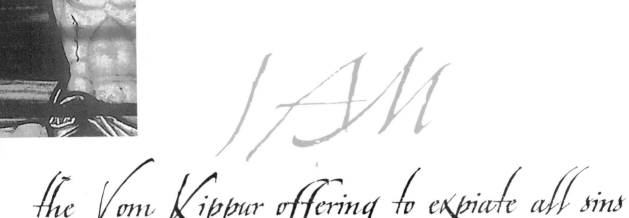

I AM

the Yom Kippur offering to expiate all sins

✜

By that will we have been sanctified
through the offering of the body of
Jesus Christ once for all.

Hebrews 10:10

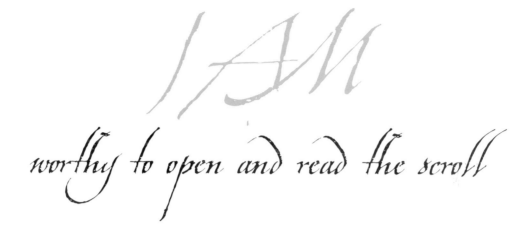

I AM

worthy to open and read the scroll

✛

So I wept much, because no one was found
worthy to open and read the scroll, or to
look at it. But one of the elders said to me,
'Do not weep. Behold, the Lion of the tribe
of Judah, the Root of David, has prevailed to
open the scroll and to loose its seven seals.'

Revelation 5:4-5

I AM

Noah's Ark in a world still filled with sin

✛

Then the Lord said to Noah,
'Come into the ark, you and all
your household, because I have
seen that you are righteous before
Me in this generation.'

Genesis 7:1

I AM

the wine and the bread

✠

And as they were eating, Jesus took bread,
blessed and broke it, and gave it to the disciples
and said, 'Take, eat; this is My body.' Then He
took the cup, and gave thanks, and gave it to
them, saying, 'Drink from it, all of you. For this is
My blood of the new covenant, which is shed for
many for the remission of sins.'

Matthew 26:26-28

I AM

alive forevermore

❖

I am He who lives, and was dead,
and behold, I am alive forevermore.
Amen. And I have the keys
of Hades and of Death.

Revelation 1:18

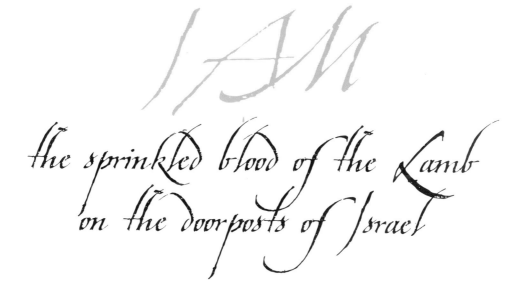

I AM

the sprinkled blood of the Lamb on the doorposts of Israel

✛

Therefore purge out the old leaven, that you may be a new lump, since you truly are unleavened. For indeed Christ, our Passover, was sacrificed for us.

1 Corinthians 5:7

111

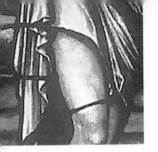

I AM

the Door to the Father

✤

Jesus said to him, 'I am the way, the
truth, and the life. No one comes to
the Father except through Me.'

John 14:6

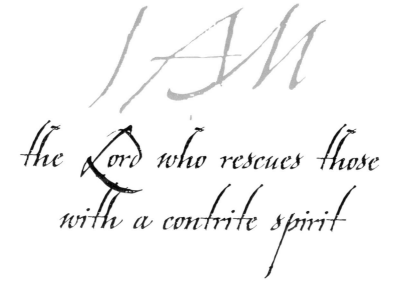

I AM

the Lord who rescues those

with a contrite spirit

✛

The Lord is near to those who have
a broken heart, and saves such as
have a contrite spirit.

Psalm 34:18

I AM

God's Son, sent to be seen face~to~face

✣

So Jacob called the name of the
place Peniel: 'For I have seen God
face-to-face, and my life is preserved.'

Genesis 32:30

I AM

He that left Heaven for you

✦

No one has ascended to heaven but He

who came down from heaven, that is,

the Son of Man who is in heaven.

John 3:13

I AM

your sanctification

✢

Speak also to the children of Israel,
saying: 'Surely My Sabbaths you shall
keep, for it is a sign between Me and
you throughout your generations, that
you may know that I am the Lord
who sanctifies you.'

Exodus 31:13

I AM

the blood atonement

✤

And not only that, but we also rejoice
in God through our Lord Jesus Christ,
through whom we have now received
the reconciliation.

Romans 5:11

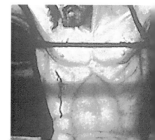

I AM

God's only Son

✣

For God so loved the world that He
gave His only begotten Son, that
whoever believes in Him should not
perish but have everlasting life.

John 3:16

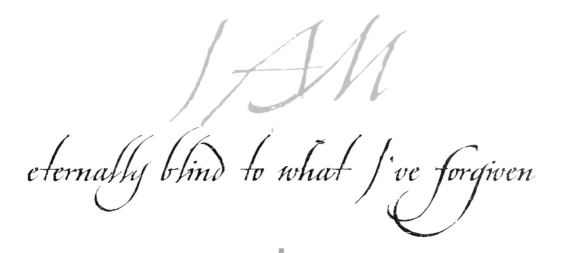

I AM

eternally blind to what I've forgiven

✠

As far as the east is from the west,

so far has He removed our

transgressions from us.

Psalm 103:12

119

I AM

the bread of life, broken for you

✚

And Jesus said to them, 'I am the
bread of life. He who comes to Me
shall never hunger, and he who
believes in Me shall never thirst.'

John 6:35

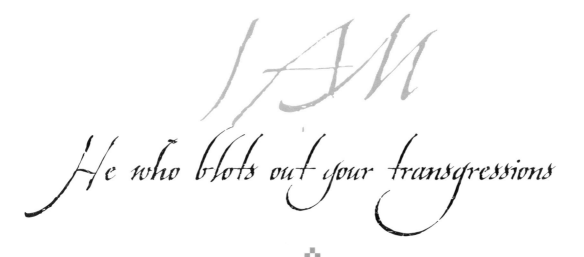

I AM

He who blots out your transgressions

✛

I, even I, am He who blots out your
transgressions for My own sake; and I
will not remember your sins.

Isaiah 43:25

121

I AM

supplication

✦

And I will pour on the house of David and on
the inhabitants of Jerusalem the Spirit of grace
and supplication; then they will look on Me
whom they pierced. Yes, they will mourn for
Him as one mourns for his only son, and
grieve for Him as one grieves for a firstborn.

Zechariah 12:10

I AM

the pierced Messiah

✛

Behold, He is coming with clouds,
and every eye will see Him,
even they who pierced Him. And all
the tribes of the earth will mourn
because of Him. Even so, Amen.

Revelation 1:7

I AM

the Keeper of the keys to Hades and death

✤

I am He who lives, and was dead,

and behold, I am alive forevermore.

Amen. And I have the keys

of Hades and of Death.

Revelation 1:18

I AM

the God of your salvation

✠

He shall receive blessing from the
Lord, and righteousness from
the God of his salvation.

Psalm 24:5

125

I AM

the Lamb that was slain

And I will pour on the house of David and on
the inhabitants of Jerusalem the Spirit of grace
and supplication; then they will look on Me
whom they pierced. Yes, they will mourn for
Him as one mourns for his only son, and
grieve for Him as one grieves for a firstborn.

Zechariah 12:10

I AM

Father, Son, and Holy Spirit

✤

For there are three that bear witness in
heaven: the Father, the Word, and the
Holy Spirit; and these three are one.

1 John 5:7

I AM

outside the camp, come to Me

✛

Therefore let us go forth to Him,

outside the camp, bearing

His reproach.

Hebrews 13:13

I AM the way, the truth, and the life

✥

Jesus said to him, 'I am the way, the
truth, and the life. No one comes to
the Father except through Me.'

John 14:6

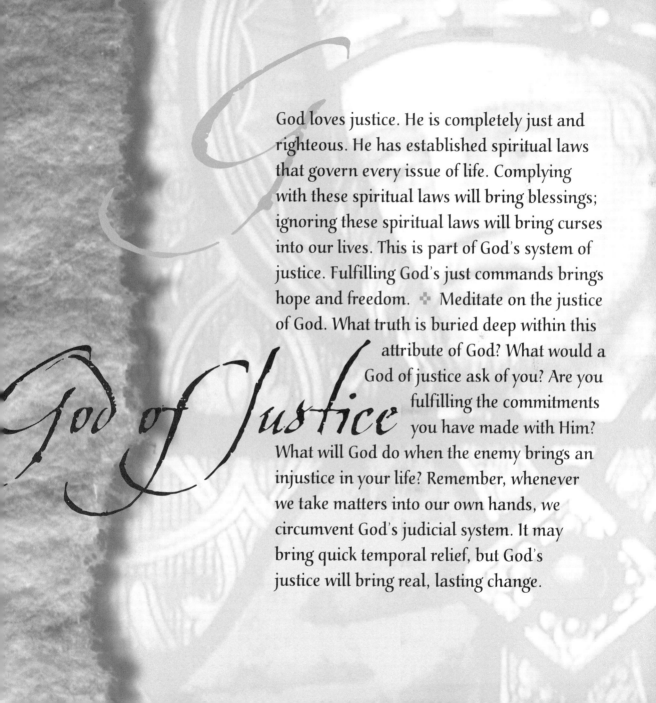

God loves justice. He is completely just and righteous. He has established spiritual laws that govern every issue of life. Complying with these spiritual laws will bring blessings; ignoring these spiritual laws will bring curses into our lives. This is part of God's system of justice. Fulfilling God's just commands brings hope and freedom. ✣ Meditate on the justice of God. What truth is buried deep within this attribute of God? What would a God of justice ask of you? Are you fulfilling the commitments you have made with Him? What will God do when the enemy brings an injustice in your life? Remember, whenever we take matters into our own hands, we circumvent God's judicial system. It may bring quick temporal relief, but God's justice will bring real, lasting change.

God of Justice

I AM

the righteous judge of all creation

✦

For He is coming to judge the earth.
With righteousness He shall judge the
world, and the peoples with equity.

Psalm 98:9

132

I AM

the King of kings

✤

And He has on His robe and on
His thigh a name written: KING OF
KINGS AND LORD OF LORDS.

Revelation 19:16

I AM

with the generation of the righteous

✦

There they are in great fear, for God is
with the generation of the righteous.

Psalm 14:5

I AM God. My statutes rejoice the heart

✜

The statutes of the Lord are
right, rejoicing the heart; the
commandment of the Lord is pure,
enlightening the eyes.

Psalm 19:8

I AM

*the One who makes unbreakable
covenants with man*

✤

And I will establish My covenant
with you. Then you shall know that
I am the Lord.

Ezekiel 16:62

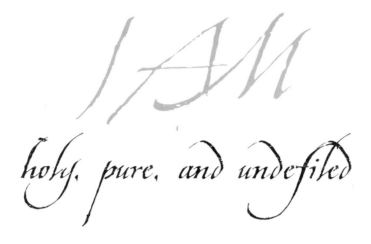

I AM

holy, pure, and undefiled

✚

For I am the Lord who brings you up
out of the land of Egypt, to be your
God. You shall therefore be holy,
for I am holy.

Leviticus 11:45

137

I AM God, besides Me there is no god

✤

Thus says the Lord, the King of Israel,
and his Redeemer, the Lord of hosts:
'I am the First and I am the Last;
besides Me there is no God.'

Isaiah 44:6

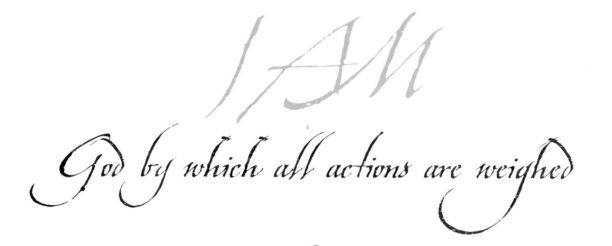

I AM

God by which all actions are weighed

✦

Talk no more so very proudly; let no
arrogance come from your mouth, for
the Lord is the God of knowledge; and
by Him actions are weighed.

1 Samuel 2:3

139

I AM

God, My testimony is sure

✛

The law of the Lord is perfect,

converting the soul; the testimony

of the Lord is sure, making

wise the simple.

Psalm 19:7

140

I AM

God. My commandments
enlighten the eyes

✚

The statutes of the Lord are
right, rejoicing the heart; the
commandment of the Lord is pure,
enlightening the eyes.

Psalm 19:8

I AM

the witness on your behalf

Then he said to them, 'The Lord is
witness against you, and His anointed
is witness this day, that you have not
found anything in my hand.' And they
answered, 'He is witness.'

1 Samuel 12:5

I AM righteous; kings humble themselves before Me

✤

So the leaders of Israel and the king
humbled themselves; and they said,
'The Lord is righteous.'

2 Chronicles 12:6

143

I AM

God whose eyelids test the sons of men

The Lord is in His holy temple,

the Lord's throne is in heaven;

His eyes behold, His eyelids test

the sons of men.

Psalm 11:4

I AM

the Spirit of wisdom

✣

The Spirit of the Lord shall rest upon
Him, the Spirit of wisdom and
understanding, the Spirit of counsel
and might, the Spirit of knowledge
and of the fear of the Lord.

Isaiah 11:2

I AM

My ordinances

✛

Therefore you shall keep My
ordinance, so that you do not commit
any of these abominable customs
which were committed before you, and
that you do not defile yourselves by
them: I am the Lord your God.

Leviticus 18:30

I AM

the divine Judge of all things

✢

Far be it from You to do such a

thing as this, to slay the righteous

with the wicked, so that the righteous

should be as the wicked; far be it from

You! Shall not the Judge of all the

earth do right?

Genesis 18:25

147

the law

For this is the covenant that I will
make with the house of Israel after
those days, says the Lord: I will put
My laws in their mind and write them
on their hearts; and I will be their
God, and they shall be My people.

Hebrews 8:10

I AM

my statutes, walk in them

✚

I am the Lord your God:

Walk in My statutes, keep My

judgments, and do them.

Ezekiel 20:19

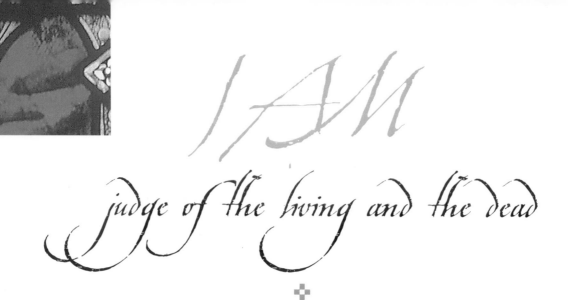

I AM

judge of the living and the dead

✛

And He commanded us to preach to
the people, and to testify that it is He
who was ordained by God to be Judge
of the living and the dead.

Acts 10:42

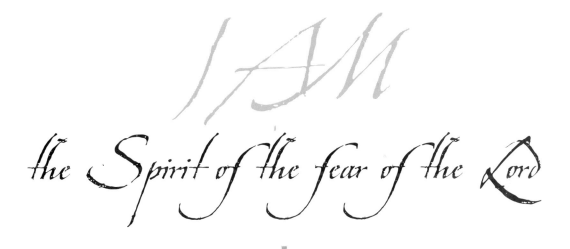

I AM
the Spirit of the fear of the Lord

✤

The Spirit of the Lord shall rest upon
Him, the Spirit of wisdom and
understanding, the Spirit of counsel
and might, the Spirit of knowledge
and of the fear of the Lord.

Isaiah 11:2

151

I AM

righteous

✚

And Pharaoh sent and called for
Moses and Aaron, and said to them,
'I have sinned this time. The Lord
is righteous, and my people and
I are wicked.'

Exodus 9:27

I AM
perfect knowledge

✦

Do you know how the clouds are
balanced, those wondrous works of
Him who is perfect in knowledge?

Job 37:16

I AM

before whom every tongue will confess

✦

'As I live,' says the Lord, 'Every knee
shall bow to Me, and every tongue
shall confess to God.'

Romans 14:11

I AM

the Lord who loves righteousness

✠

For the Lord is righteous, He loves

righteousness; His countenance

beholds the upright.

Psalm 11:7

I AM

the unbiased, impartial judge

✦

Far be it from You to do such a
thing as this, to slay the righteous
with the wicked, so that the righteous
should be as the wicked; far be it from
You! Shall not the Judge of all the
earth do right?

Genesis 18:25

156

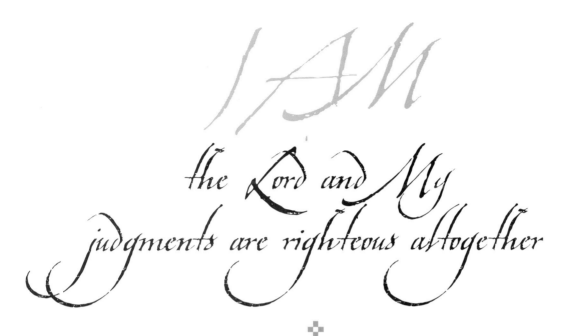

I AM the Lord and My judgments are righteous altogether

❖

The fear of the Lord is clean, enduring
forever; the judgments of the Lord are
true and righteous altogether.

Psalm 19:9

157

I AM

He who sent Moses to deliver Israel

✛

And God said to Moses,
'I AM WHO I AM.' And He said, 'Thus
you shall say to the children of Israel,
'I AM has sent me to you.'

Exodus 3:14

I AM

God and no one can reverse My acts

✦

Indeed before the day was, I am He;
and there is no one who can deliver
out of My hand; I work, and who
will reverse it?

Isaiah 43:13

159

I AM
to be feared above all gods

✤

For the Lord is great and greatly
to be praised; He is also to be
feared above all gods.

1 Chronicles 16:25

_I AM_

God who refines you

✛

Behold, I have refined you, but not
as silver; I have tested you in the
furnace of affliction.

Isaiah 48:10

I AM

My judgments

✤

You shall therefore keep My
statutes and My judgments,
which if a man does, he shall live
by them: I am the Lord.

Leviticus 18:5

I AM
the Lord who heals you

✠

...If you diligently heed the voice of the Lord
your God and do what is right in His sight, give
ear to His commandments and keep all His
statutes, I will put none of the diseases on you
which I have brought on the Egyptians.
For I am the Lord who heals you.

Exodus 15:26

163

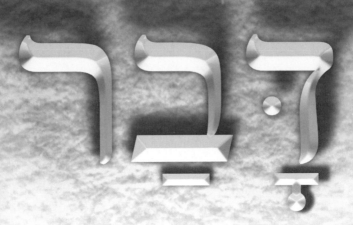

Following God isn't always easy. However, any difficulty we face is softened by the fact that God has made deep and specific promises to His creation. His promises range from the most visible expressions of His power to the most intimate moments with us. ✤ Meditate on the promises God has made you. What does God desire for you? What did He whisper to you in your childhood? What dreams did He give you in your teenage years? What promises has He made to you in the past few years? What more does God want to give you? ✤ Consider what you are doing that will hinder God's promises from being fulfilled in your life. Do you realize that you can frustrate the grace of God and hinder God's desires from being displayed in your life?

God of Promise

I AM

returning

✛

And if I go and prepare a place
for you, I will come again and
receive you to Myself; that where
I am, there you may be also.

John 14:3

I AM

God and I want you to believe in Me

✠

'You are My witnesses,' says the Lord,
'and My servant whom I have chosen,
that you may know and believe Me,
and understand that I am He. Before
Me there was no God formed, nor
shall there be after Me.'

Isaiah 43:10

167

I AM

He who places your tears in My bottle, in My book

✤

You number my wanderings;

put my tears into Your bottle;

are they not in Your book?

Psalm 56:8

I AM
God who shows you things to come

✛

However, when He, the Spirit of truth,
has come, He will guide you into all
truth; for He will not speak on His
own authority, but whatever He
hears He will speak; and He will
tell you things to come.

John 16:13

I AM

the seven Spirits and they are Me

✛

And from the throne proceeded
lightnings, thunderings, and voices.
Seven lamps of fire were burning
before the throne, which are the
seven Spirits of God.

Revelation 4:5

*I AM
the Lord, the fear of Me
is a fountain of life*

✤

The fear of the Lord is a fountain
of life, to turn one away from
the snares of death.

Proverbs 14:27

171

I AM

God. My secrets are with those who fear Me

✠

The secret of the Lord is with those

who fear Him, and He will show

them His covenant.

Psalm 25:14

172

I AM

life's guarantor of joy and health

✛

Behold, I will bring it health
and healing; I will heal them and
reveal to them the abundance
of peace and truth.

Jeremiah 33:6

173

I AM

God who will be found by those who seek Me with all their heart and soul

But from there you will seek the
Lord your God, and you will find
Him if you seek Him with all your
heart and with all your soul.

Deuteronomy 4:29

I AM

and you shall know My names

✛

Therefore My people shall

know My name.

Isaiah 52:6a

175

I AM

He who leads you in the paths of righteousness

✛

He restores my soul; He leads
me in the paths of righteousness
for His name's sake.

Psalm 23:3

I AM

the architect of the last days

✛

God, who at various times and in
various ways spoke in time past to the
fathers by the prophets, has in these
last days spoken to us by His Son.

Hebrews 1:1-2

177

I AM

the sole key giver of Heaven

✦

And I will give you the keys of the
kingdom of heaven, and whatever you
bind on earth will be bound in
heaven, and whatever you loose on
earth will be loosed in heaven.

Matthew 16:19

178

I AM

the God who hears

✦

For that is his only covering, it is
his garment for his skin. What will
he sleep in? And it will be that when
he cries to Me, I will hear,
for I am gracious.

Exodus 22:27

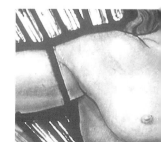

I AM

the Lord who hears those who speak about My name

✚

Then those who feared the Lord spoke to one another, and the Lord listened and heard them; so a book of remembrance was written before Him for those who fear the Lord and who meditate on His name.

Malachi 3:16

180

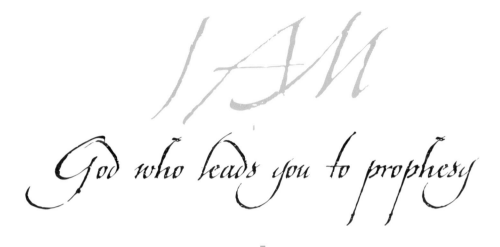

_I AM_

God who leads you to prophesy

✛

'And it shall come to pass in the last
days,' says God, 'that I will pour out of
My Spirit on all flesh; your sons and
your daughters shall prophesy, your
young men shall see visions, your old
men shall dream dreams.'

Acts 2:17

181

I AM

the soon~coming King

✦

Then the seventh angel sounded:
And there were loud voices in heaven,
saying, 'The kingdoms of this world
have become the kingdoms of our
Lord and of His Christ, and He shall
reign forever and ever!'

Revelation 11:15

the Lord, I do not change

✚

For I am the Lord, I do not change;

therefore you are not consumed,

O sons of Jacob.

Malachi 3:6

183

always with you, wherever you are

I am with you always,

even to the end of the age.

Matthew 28:20b

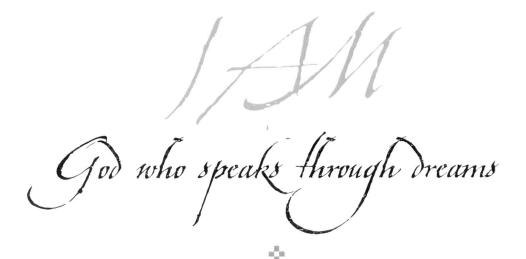

I AM

God who speaks through dreams

✛

Then He said, 'If there is a prophet
among you, I, the Lord, make Myself
known to him in a vision; I speak
to him in a dream.'

Numbers 12:6

185

I AM

God who reveals His form

✤

I speak with him face to face, even
plainly, and not in dark sayings; and
he sees the form of the Lord. Why then
were you not afraid to speak against
My servant Moses?

Numbers 12:8

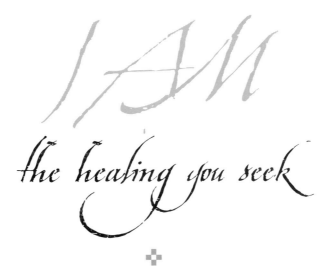

I AM

the healing you seek

✦

But He was wounded for our
transgressions, He was bruised for our
iniquities; the chastisement for our
peace was upon Him, and by His
stripes we are healed.

Isaiah 53:5

187

I AM

the Savior who will descend on the Mount of Olives

✤

And in that day His feet will stand on the Mount of Olives, which faces Jerusalem on the east. And the Mount of Olives shall be split in two, from east to west, making a very large valley; half of the mountain shall move toward the north and half of it toward the south.

Zechariah 14:4

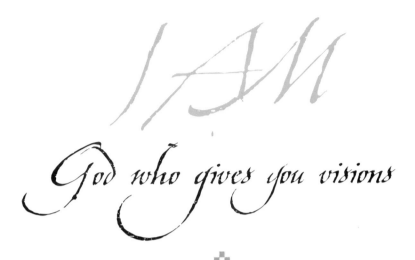

I AM

God who gives you visions

✛

'And it shall come to pass in the last
days,' says God, 'that I will pour out of
My Spirit on all flesh; your sons and
your daughters shall prophesy, your
young men shall see visions, your old
men shall dream dreams.'

Acts 2:17

I AM

God of those who are growing old

✠

Even to your old age, I am He, and
even to gray hairs I will carry you!
I have made, and I will bear; even I
will carry, and will deliver you.

Isaiah 46:4

I AM
coming quickly

✛

Behold, I am coming quickly!
Hold fast what you have, that
no one may take your crown.

Revelation 3:11

191

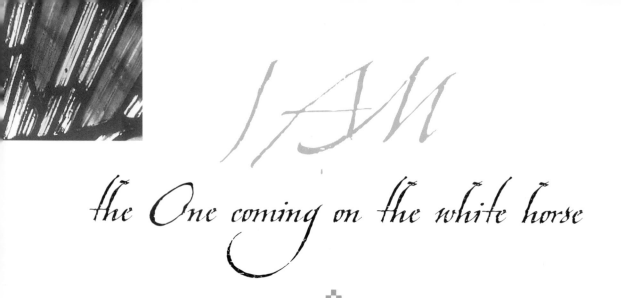

I AM

the One coming on the white horse

✛

Now I saw heaven opened, and
behold, a white horse. And He who sat
on him was called Faithful and True,
and in righteousness He judges
and makes war.

Revelation 19:11

192

I AM

the soon rending of the Heavens

✠

Oh, that You would rend the heavens!

That You would come down!

Isaiah 64:1a

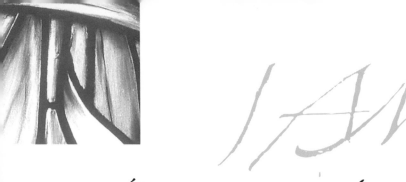

I AM

the precision of My Scripture

✜

All Scripture is given by inspiration
of God, and is profitable for doctrine,
for reproof, for correction, for
instruction in righteousness. . .

2 Timothy 3:16

I AM

waiting for you

✛

Therefore the Lord will wait, that

He may be gracious to you.

Isaiah 30:18a

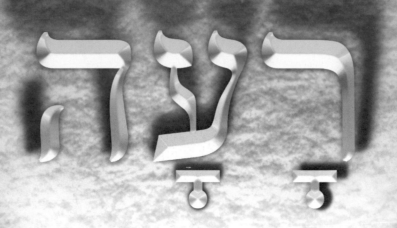

God the Shepherd

Like any good shepherd, God is protective of His sheep. Scripture tells us that we are His sheep. As such, He wants to keep us safe and cared for. ❖ Picture yourself as a lamb in Jesus' arms, frail and weak, but safe in His care. Ask God for His protection. Ask Him to guide you through your day and in your decisions. Ask for the tender care of your loving Father. ❖ In Psalm 23, we discover that sometimes God makes us lie down and be still. Sometimes, He leads us by the still waters to restore our soul. Sometimes, we have to trust Him to make a table for us in the presence of our enemies. Sometimes, we have to let God shepherd us.

I AM

your shepherd, you shall not want

✤

The Lord is my shepherd;

I shall not want.

Psalm 23:1

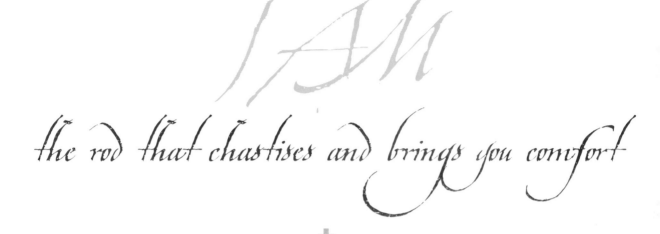

I AM the rod that chastises and brings you comfort

✤

Yea, though I walk through the valley
of the shadow of death, I will fear no
evil; for You are with me; Your rod and
Your staff, they comfort me.

Psalm 23:4

I AM

in the desert wilderness to be
tender with you

✛

Therefore, behold, I will allure her,

will bring her into the wilderness,

and speak comfort to her.

Hosea 2:14

I AM

near to those who have a broken heart

✛

The Lord is near to those who have
a broken heart, and saves such as
have a contrite spirit.

Psalm 34:18

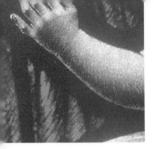

I AM

your confidence

✤

For the Lord will be your
confidence, and will keep your
foot from being caught.

Proverbs 3:26

I AM

compassion

✦

The Lord is gracious and full of
compassion, slow to anger
and great in mercy.

Psalm 145:8

I AM

in the Father

✛

Believe Me that I am in the Father and
the Father in Me, or else believe Me
for the sake of the works themselves.

John 14:11

I AM with you and will keep you wherever you go

✣

Behold, I am with you and will keep
you wherever you go, and will bring
you back to this land; for I will not
leave you until I have done what
I have spoken to you.

Genesis 28:15

I AM

the refuge of the poor

✛

You shame the counsel of the poor,

but the Lord is his refuge.

Psalm 14:6

I AM

your Father

✛

Do not call anyone on earth your
father; for One is your Father,
He who is in heaven.

Matthew 23:9

I AM

God in the stillness

✠

Be still, and know that I am God;

I will be exalted among the nations,

I will be exalted in the earth!

Psalm 46:10

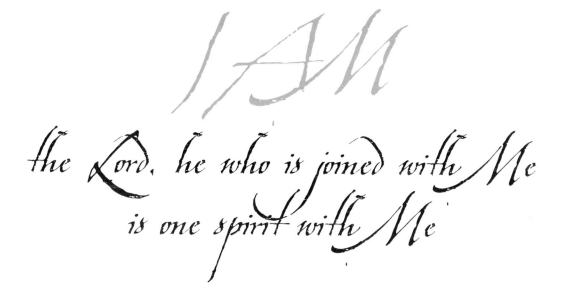

I AM the Lord, he who is joined with Me is one spirit with Me

✢

But he who is joined to the Lord
is one spirit with Him.

1 Corinthians 6:17

I AM

the Spirit of counsel

✛

The Spirit of the Lord shall rest upon
Him, the Spirit of wisdom and
understanding, the Spirit of counsel
and might, the Spirit of knowledge
and of the fear of the Lord.

Isaiah 11:2

210

I AM

your provider

✠

Then Abraham lifted his eyes and looked, and there behind him was a ram caught in a thicket by its horns. So Abraham went and took the ram, and offered it up for a burnt offering instead of his son. And Abraham called the name of the place, The-Lord-Will-Provide; as it is said to this day, 'In the Mount of the Lord it shall be provided.'

Genesis 22:13-14

211

I AM

tenderness

Remember, O Lord, Your tender
mercies and Your lovingkindnesses,
for they are from of old.

Psalm 25:6

I AM

the true shepherd

✣

I am the good shepherd; and I know
My sheep, and am known by My own.

John 10:14

I AM
the dispeller of all fear and doubt

✛

Fear not, for I am with you; be not
dismayed, for I am your God. I will
strengthen you, yes, I will help you,
I will uphold you with My
righteous right hand.

Isaiah 41:10

214

I AM

interceding for you right now

✣

Now He who searches the hearts
knows what the mind of the Spirit is,
because He makes intercession for the
saints according to the will of God.

Romans 8:27

215

I AM

love

✛

He who does not love does not
know God, for God is love.

1 John 4:8

I AM

the staff that retrieves you

✤

Yea, though I walk through the valley
of the shadow of death, I will fear no
evil; for You are with me; Your rod and
Your staff, they comfort me.

Psalm 23:4

I AM

man's friend who sticks closer than a brother

✦

A man who has friends must himself
be friendly, but there is a friend who
sticks closer than a brother.

Proverbs 18:24

218

I AM

the shepherd's rod

✛

Yea, though I walk through the valley
of the shadow of death, I will fear no
evil; for You are with me; Your rod and
Your staff, they comfort me.

Psalm 23:4

I AM

*God who is with you in the valley
of the shadow of death*

✛

Fear not, for I am with you; be not
dismayed, for I am your God. I will
strengthen you, yes, I will help you,
I will uphold you with My
righteous right hand.

Isaiah 41:10

I AM

there with you

✦

But they said, 'We have certainly
seen that the Lord is with you.'

Genesis 26:28a

I AM

God who strengthens you

✠

I can do all things

through Christ

who strengthens me.

Philippians 4:13

I AM

the candle lighting your path

✦

For You will light my lamp; the Lord
my God will enlighten my darkness.

Psalm 18:28

223

I AM the Lord; precious in My sight is the death of all My saints

✠

Precious in the sight of the Lord is

the death of His saints.

Psalm 116:15

224

I AM

the Counselor, Mighty God, Everlasting Father

✢

For unto us a Child is born, unto us a Son is given;
and the government will be upon His shoulder. And
His name will be called Wonderful, Counselor,
Mighty God, Everlasting Father, Prince of Peace.

Isaiah 9:6

225

I AM

your peace and calm

✣

For He Himself is our peace, who has
made both one, and has broken down
the middle wall of separation. . .

Ephesians 2:14

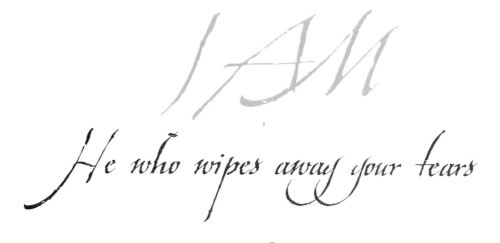

I AM

He who wipes away your tears

✦

He will swallow up death forever, and
the Lord God will wipe away tears
from all faces; the rebuke of His
people He will take away from all the
earth; for the Lord has spoken.

Isaiah 25:8

227

I AM

the saving refuge of My anointed

✠

The Lord is their strength, and He is
the saving refuge of His anointed.

Psalm 28:8

God the Ancient One

Before the world existed, God was. Brooding over the darkness, He created everything we know that exists. After forming the earth and creating light, God created mankind. Our ancient forefathers, Adam, Abel, Enoch, Noah, Abraham, Isaac, and Jacob, heard God's voice, responded to Him, and discovered the promises contained in His wonderful names and attributes. ✤ The Ancient of Days made promises to our forefathers, and made covenants with them that have lasted unto this day. He wanted men and women to spread the fragrance of His name throughout the earth. ✤ Ponder the Lord's ancient ways. Ask Him to renew the ancient covenants made with your forefathers. Ask God to restore the blessings of your forefathers. Ask Him to release to you the unfulfilled promises of your forefathers and the blessings they did not grasp. What they did not claim is still available to you today.

I AM

the Lord God of Abraham, Isaac, and Jacob

✛

Moreover He said, 'I am the God of
your father - the God of Abraham, the
God of Isaac, and the God of Jacob.'
And Moses hid his face, for he was
afraid to look upon God.

Exodus 3:6

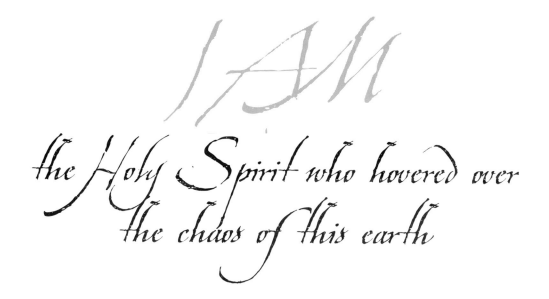

I AM

the Holy Spirit who hovered over
the chaos of this earth

✢

The earth was without form, and void;
and darkness was on the face of the
deep. And the Spirit of God was
hovering over the face of the waters.

Genesis 1:2

I AM

the light of Genesis that was
before light was

❖

Then God said, 'Let there be light';

and there was light.

Genesis 1:3

I AM

the sacred Shema of the ancients

✦

Sh'ma Israel, Adonai Eloheynu,

Adonai echad!

(An ancient prayer translated:

Hear, O Israel: The Lord our God,

the Lord is one!)

Deuteronomy 6:4

I AM
the Holy One of Israel

✠

For I am the Lord your God, the Holy
One of Israel, your Savior.

Isaiah 43:3a

I AM

the One whose ways are perfect

✛

As for God, His way is perfect; the
word of the Lord is proven; He is a
shield to all who trust in Him.

2 Samuel 22:31

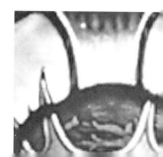

I AM

God, the fear of Me is clean,
enduring forever

✦

The fear of the Lord is clean, enduring
forever; the judgments of the Lord are
true and righteous altogether.

Psalm 19:9

I AM
the Holy of Holies

✤

Then the priests brought in the ark of
the covenant of the Lord to its place,
into the inner sanctuary of the temple,
to the Most Holy Place, under the
wings of the cherubim.

1 Kings 8:6

239

I AM
the God of knowledge

✛

Talk no more so very proudly; let no
arrogance come from your mouth, for
the Lord is the God of knowledge; and
by Him actions are weighed.

1 Samuel 2:3

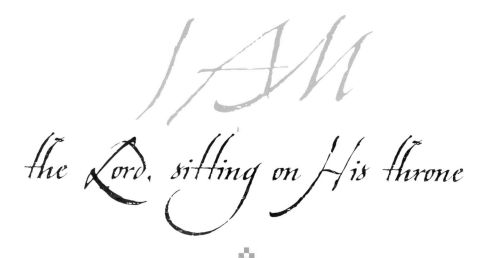

I AM the Lord, sitting on His throne

✤

In the year that King Uzziah died,
I saw the Lord sitting on a throne,
high and lifted up, and the train of
His robe filled the temple.

Isaiah 6:1

241

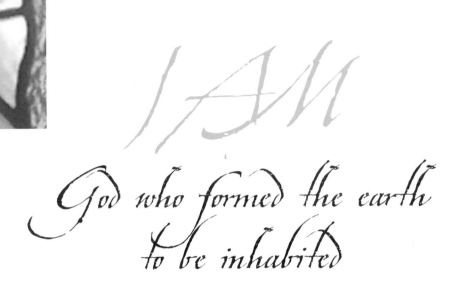

I AM

God who formed the earth to be inhabited

✦

For thus says the Lord, who created the heavens,
who is God, who formed the earth and made it,
who has established it, who did not create it in
vain, who formed it to be inhabited: 'I am the
Lord, and there is no other.'

Isaiah 45:18

I AM

understanding

✤

But there is a spirit in man, and
the breath of the Almighty gives
him understanding.

Job 32:8

I AM

God who is joined to the eunuch

✦

Do not let the son of the foreigner who
has joined himself to the Lord speak,
saying, 'The Lord has utterly separated
me from His people'; nor let the
eunuch say, 'Here I am, a dry tree.'

Isaiah 56:3

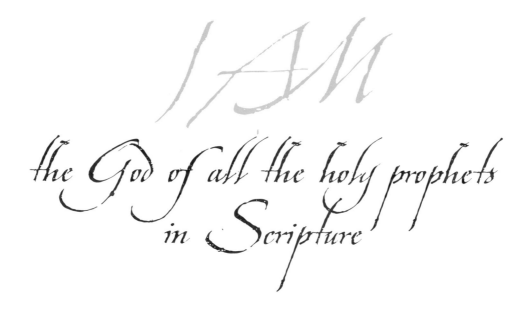

I AM
the God of all the holy prophets in Scripture

✠

Then he said to me, 'These words are
faithful and true.' And the Lord God of
the holy prophets sent His angel to
show His servants the things which
must shortly take place.

Revelation 22:6

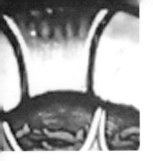

I AM

God who divided the sea

✠

But I am the Lord your God, who

divided the sea whose waves roared -

the Lord of hosts is His name.

Isaiah 51:15

I AM

the Lord of the dance

✛

Let them praise His name
with the dance.

Psalm 149:3a

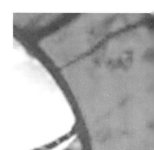

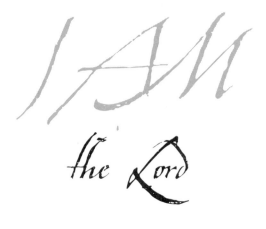

I AM

the Lord

✤

And God spoke to Moses and said

to him: 'I am the Lord.'

Exodus 6:2

I AM
the guiding star at Jesus' birth

✛

When they heard the king, they departed; and
behold, the star which they had seen in the East
went before them, till it came and stood over
where the young Child was. When they saw the
star, they rejoiced with exceedingly great joy.

Matthew 2:9-10

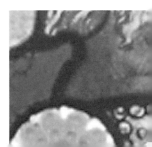

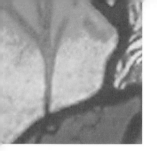

I AM

God who turns water into wine

✦

Jesus said to them, 'Fill the waterpots with water.' And they
filled them up to the brim. And He said to them, 'Draw
some out now, and take it to the master of the feast.' And
they took it. When the master of the feast had tasted the
water that was made wine, and did not know where it came
from (but the servants who had drawn the water knew), the
master of the feast called the bridegroom.

John 2:7-9

250

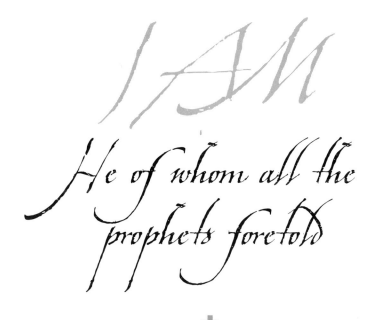

I AM

He of whom all the prophets foretold

Philip found Nathanael and said to him, 'We have found Him of whom Moses in the law, and also the prophets, wrote - Jesus of Nazareth, the son of Joseph.'

John 1:45

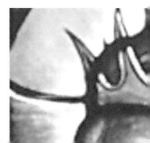

I AM

the Root of the Offspring of David

✦

I, Jesus, have sent My angel to testify
to you these things in the churches. I
am the Root and the Offspring of
David, the Bright and Morning Star.

Revelation 22:16

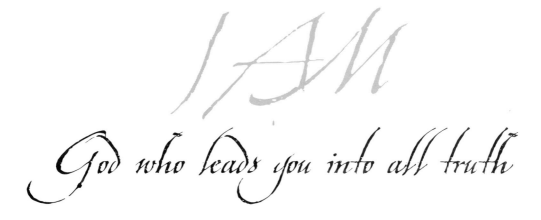

I AM

God who leads you into all truth

✠

However, when He, the Spirit of truth, has
come, He will guide you into all truth; for
He will not speak on His own authority,
but whatever He hears He will speak; and
He will tell you things to come.

John 16:13

253

I AM

God, whose rainbow is My everlasting covenant with you

✛

The rainbow shall be in the cloud,
and I will look on it to remember the
everlasting covenant between God
and every living creature of all
flesh that is on the earth.

Genesis 9:16

254

I AM
the Root of Jesse

✛

And in that day there shall be a
Root of Jesse, who shall stand as a
banner to the people; for the Gentiles
shall seek Him, and His resting
place shall be glorious.

Isaiah 11:10

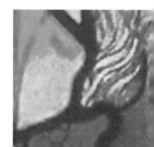

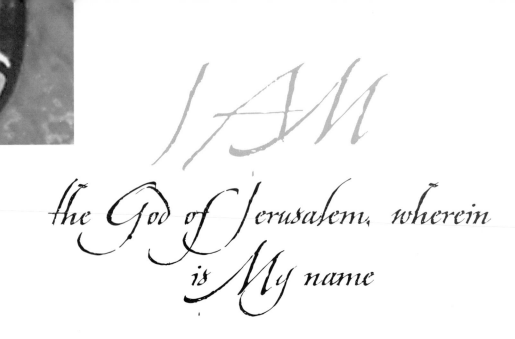

I AM

the God of Jerusalem, wherein
is My name

✣

He also built altars in the house of the
Lord, of which the Lord had said, 'In
Jerusalem I will put My name.'

2 Kings 21:4

I AM
the Creator of Israel

✛

I am the Lord, your Holy One,
the Creator of Israel, your King.

Isaiah 43:15

I AM
the God who divided the waters

✛

Then Moses stretched out his hand
over the sea; and the Lord caused the
sea to go back by a strong east wind
all that night, and made the sea into
dry land, and the waters were divided.

Exodus 14:21

I AM

the fountain of the house of David

✣

In that day a fountain shall be
opened for the house of David and
for the inhabitants of Jerusalem,
for sin and for uncleanness.

Zechariah 13:1

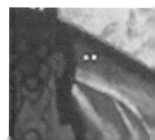

I AM

God who shuts up the Heavens

✛

. . . lest the Lord's anger be aroused
against you, and He shut up the
heavens so that there be no rain, and
the land yield no produce, and you
perish quickly from the good land
which the Lord is giving you.

Deuteronomy 11:17

I AM

God who turns water into blood

✛

And the Egyptians shall know that I
am the Lord, when I stretch out My
hand on Egypt and bring out the
children of Israel from among them.

Exodus 7:5

261

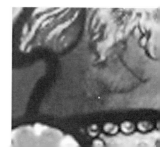

I AM

married to Israel

✛

Go and proclaim these words toward
the north, and say: 'Return,
backsliding Israel,' says the Lord; 'I
will not cause My anger to fall on you.
For I am merciful,' says the Lord; 'I
will not remain angry forever.'

Jeremiah 3:12

God loves to lavish great gifts on His servants. He loves to reward us for our faithfulness and righteous acts. In fact, He promises to give us every good and every perfect gift (James 1:17). What an intimate portrait of God's compassion, loving-kindness, and majesty. ✤ Being with God for an eternity, seeing Him face-to-face, is our exceedingly great reward for a life well-lived (Genesis 15:1). ✤ Consider God's characteristics that give you the most joy. What is it about His attributes that you long to enjoy for eternity? What do you want to wholeheartedly embrace in Him? Remember to drink deeply from the Lord, the Fountain of life, who is your exceedingly great reward. ✤ Study the promises made to the seven churches listed in Revelation 2 and 3. Ask God to give you the rewards He promises to those who overcome.

God the Reward

I AM

your exceedingly great reward

✛

After these things the word of the Lord
came to Abram in a vision, saying, 'Do
not be afraid, Abram. I am your
shield, your exceedingly great reward.'

Genesis 15:1

266

I AM the Lord, taste and see that I am good

Oh, taste and see that the
Lord is good; blessed is the
man who trusts in Him!

Psalm 34:8

I AM
both the giver and the gifts

✤

Every good gift and every perfect gift
is from above, and comes down from
the Father of lights, with whom there
is no variation or shadow of turning.

James 1:17

I AM

the preparer of your place in Heaven

✠

And if I go and prepare a place for
you, I will come again and receive
you to Myself; that where I am,
there you may be also.

John 14:3

I AM

able to give you much more than this

Then Amaziah said to the man of God,
'But what shall we do about the
hundred talents which I have given to
the troops of Israel?' And the man of
God answered, 'The Lord is able to
give you much more than this.'

2 Chronicles 25:9

270

I AM

the one source of all true wealth

✛

Every good gift and every perfect gift is
from above, and comes down from the
Father of lights, with whom there is no
variation or shadow of turning.

James 1:17

271

I AM
the Spirit of liberty

✥

Now the Lord is the Spirit;
and where the Spirit of the Lord is,
there is liberty.

2 Corinthians 3:17

I AM

He who anoints your head with oil

✜

You prepare a table before me in the
presence of my enemies; You anoint
my head with oil; my cup runs over.

Psalm 23:5

273

I AM
the Bridegroom returning for My bride

✦

And the Spirit and the bride say,
'Come!' And let him who hears say,
'Come!' And let him who thirsts come.
Whoever desires, let him take the
water of life freely.

Revelation 22:17

274

I AM

the Lord who looks on those who tremble at My Word

✦

'For all those things My hand has
made, and all those things exist,' says
the Lord. 'But on this one will I look:
On him who is poor and of a contrite
spirit, and who trembles at My word.'

Isaiah 66:2

I AM

*God who prepares a table for you
in the presence of your enemies*

✚

You prepare a table before me in the
presence of my enemies; You anoint
my head with oil; my cup runs over.

Psalm 23:5

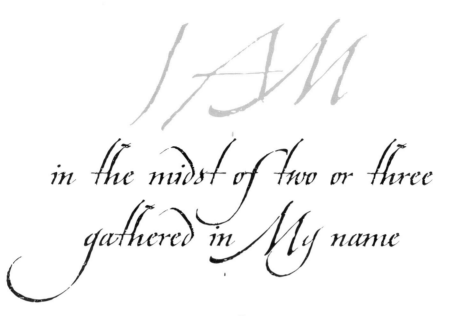

I AM in the midst of two or three gathered in My name

✤

For where two or three are gathered
together in My name, I am there
in the midst of them.

Matthew 18:20

277

I AM

God who will answer you

✛

Then you shall call, and the Lord will
answer; you shall cry, and He will say,
'Here I am.'

Isaiah 58:9a

I AM

the glory who conceals a matter
for a king to search out

✦

It is the glory of God to conceal a
matter, but the glory of kings is to
search out a matter.

Proverbs 25:2

I AM
the fountain of gardens

✜

. . .a fountain of gardens,
a well of living waters,
and streams from Lebanon.

Song of Solomon 4:15

I AM the resurrection of My beloved

✤

Jesus said to her, 'I am the
resurrection and the life. He who
believes in Me, though he may die,
he shall live.'

John 11:25

I AM
God whose throne is in Heaven

The Lord is in His holy temple,

the Lord's throne is in heaven;

His eyes behold, His eyelids test

the sons of men.

Psalm 11:4

I AM

from above

✜

And He said to them, 'You are from
beneath; I am from above. You are of
this world; I am not of this world.'

John 8:23

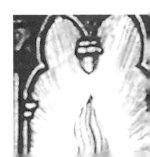

I AM

the Lord whose countenance
beholds the upright

✣

For the Lord is righteous, He loves

righteousness; His countenance

beholds the upright.

Psalm 11:7

I AM

the just rewarder of all who seek Me

✤

But without faith it is impossible
to please Him, for he who comes to
God must believe that He is,
and that He is a rewarder of those
who diligently seek Him.

Hebrews 11:6

I AM

God who teaches you to profit

✛

Thus says the Lord, your Redeemer,

the Holy One of Israel:

'I am the Lord your God,

who teaches you to profit, who leads

you by the way you should go.'

Isaiah 48:17

I AM

the giver of abundant life

✢

The thief does not come except
to steal, and to kill, and to destroy.
I have come that they may have life,
and that they may have it
more abundantly.

John 10:10

287

I AM

more than you can ask or think

✤

For as the heavens are higher
than the earth, so are My ways
higher than your ways, and My
thoughts than your thoughts.

Isaiah 55:9

I AM

sitting at the right hand of the Father

✛

Jesus said, 'I am. And you will see
the Son of Man sitting at the right
hand of the Power, and coming
with the clouds of heaven.'

Mark 14:62

289

I AM

the Maker of many mansions therein

✠

In My Father's house are many
mansions; if it were not so, I would
have told you. I go to prepare
a place for you.

John 14:2

I AM
the Sabbath rest

✠

Therefore the Son of Man
is also Lord of the Sabbath.

Mark 2:28

I AM

the inheritance of the Levite

✦

The priests, the Levites - all the tribe of Levi -
shall have no part nor inheritance with Israel;
they shall eat the offerings of the Lord made by
fire, and His portion. Therefore they shall have
no inheritance among their brethren; the Lord
is their inheritance, as He said to them.

Deuteronomy 18:1-2

I AM

the fountain of life

✛

The fear of the Lord is a
fountain of life, to turn one
away from the snares of death.

Proverbs 14:27

I AM

the giver of great wisdom

✤

If any of you lacks wisdom,
let him ask of God, who gives to all
liberally and without reproach,
and it will be given to him.

James 1:5

I AM

the Holy Spirit that hovers over
your life to bring higher order

✛

As an eagle stirs up its nest, hovers over

its young, spreading out its wings, taking

them up, carrying them on its wings,

so the Lord alone led him.

Deuteronomy 32:11-12

God the Warrior

When God makes a covenant, He is forcefully protective of that promise. So when God chose Israel as His people, the nation's enemies knew God would protect that culture. And He did. ✤ Throughout the ages, God has obliterated the enemies of His chosen people. Today, in our nation, the enemies of His people are spiritual ones, not flesh and blood, but powers and principalities. God wars with those demonic forces, shattering their power and bringing His Kingdom to earth. Jesus Christ, through His magnificent sacrifice on the Cross, has already won this battle. ✤ Take time, as Moses did in Exodus 17:15, to build a symbolic altar in your life commemorating the victories Christ has won for you. Moses called his altar "The-Lord-Is-My-Banner." God has a special battle standard He wants to share with you. Ask Him for it.

I AM

the battle standard

So shall they fear the name of the Lord
from the west, and His glory from the
rising of the sun; when the enemy comes
in like a flood, the Spirit of the Lord will
lift up a standard against him.

Isaiah 59:19

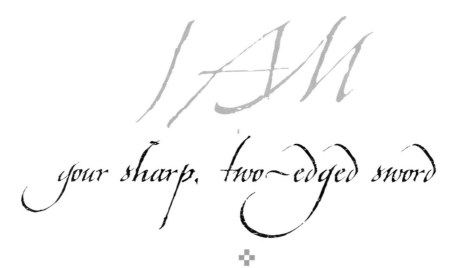

I AM

your sharp, two-edged sword

✤

And to the angel of the church in
Pergamos write, 'These things says He
who has the sharp two-edged sword.

Revelation 2:12

299

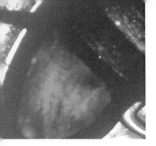

I AM

your battle cry

✜

So the people shouted when the priests blew the
trumpets. And it happened when the people heard
the sound of the trumpet, and the people shouted
with a great shout, that the wall fell down flat.
Then the people went up into the city, every man
straight before him, and they took the city.

Joshua 6:20

300

I AM a warrior and My Kingdom is spread by force

✦

The Lord is a man of war;

the Lord is His name.

Exodus 15:3

301

I AM

the Lord mighty in battle

✠

Who is this King of glory?

The Lord strong and mighty,

the Lord mighty in battle.

Psalm 24:8

I AM

the One who annihilated Satan's plans

✜

And the God of peace will crush
Satan under your feet shortly.

Romans 16:20a

I AM

the Spirit of might

✢

The Spirit of the Lord shall rest upon
Him, the Spirit of wisdom and
understanding, the Spirit of counsel
and might, the Spirit of knowledge
and of the fear of the Lord.

Isaiah 11:2

I AM

the master planner of all nations

and kingdoms

✣

For the kingdom is the Lord's,
and He rules over the nations.

Psalm 22:28

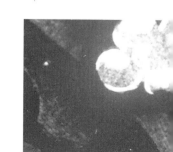

305

I AM

He who leads you for My

great name's sake

✧

He restores my soul; He leads

me in the paths of righteousness

for His name's sake.

Psalm 23:3

I AM

the conqueror of death, hell, and the grave

✠

O Death, where is your sting? O
Hades, where is your victory? But
thanks be to God, who gives us the
victory through our Lord Jesus Christ.

1 Corinthians 15:55, 57

I AM

both warrior and poet

✛

My heart is overflowing with a good
theme; I recite my composition
concerning the King; my tongue is
the pen of a ready writer.

Psalm 45:1

I AM

the Supreme God, deliverer, and possessor

✤

And blessed be God Most High,
who has delivered your enemies
into your hand.

Genesis 14:20a

I AM
the Lord of Hosts

✦

Then Micaiah said, 'Therefore hear
the word of the Lord: I saw the Lord
sitting on His throne, and all the host
of heaven standing by, on His right
hand and on His left.'

1 Kings 22:19

I AM

the Kingdom, the power, and the glory

✛

And do not lead us into temptation,
but deliver us from the evil one.
For Yours is the kingdom and the
power and the glory forever.

Matthew 6:13

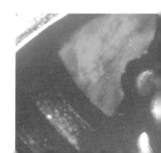

I AM

God who cast out nations before you

✛

Do not defile yourselves with any of
these things; for by all these the
nations are defiled, which I am casting
out before you.

Leviticus 18:24

I AM

commander-in-chief of all Heaven's armies

✤

And the armies in heaven, clothed
in fine linen, white and clean,
followed Him on white horses.

Revelation 19:14

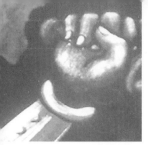

I AM

He who drives out the wicked before you

✛

Do not think in your heart, after the Lord your
God has cast them out before you, saying,
'Because of my righteousness the Lord has
brought me in to possess this land'; but it is
because of the wickedness of these nations that
the Lord is driving them out from before you.

Deuteronomy 9:4

I AM

the defender of those who believe in Me

✛

My defense is of God, who
saves the upright in heart.

Psalm 7:10

315

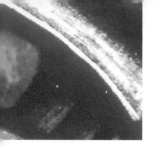

I AM

your strength

✠

The Lord is my strength and song, and
He has become my salvation; He is my
God, and I will praise Him; my
father's God, and I will exalt Him.

Exodus 15:2

I AM
the Lamb sitting on the throne

✤

. . .for the Lamb who is in the midst of
the throne will shepherd them and
lead them to living fountains of
waters. And God will wipe away every
tear from their eyes.

Revelation 7:17

317

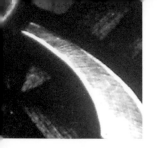

I AM

your victorious banner

And Moses built an altar and called
its name, The-Lord-Is-My-Banner.

Exodus 17:15

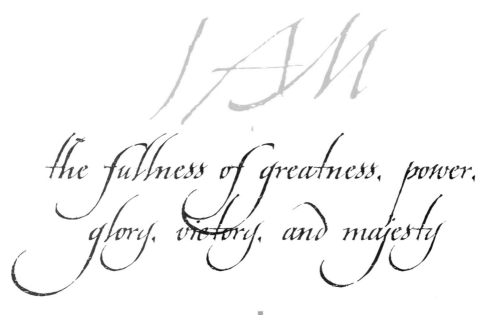

I AM

the fullness of greatness, power,
glory, victory, and majesty

✦

Yours, O Lord, is the greatness, the power
and the glory, the victory and the majesty;
for all that is in heaven and in earth is
Yours; Yours is the kingdom, O Lord, and
You are exalted as head over all.

1 Chronicles 29:11

319

I AM

God Almighty and infinite in strength

✠

Also God said to him: 'I am God
Almighty. Be fruitful and multiply; a
nation and a company of nations shall
proceed from you, and kings shall
come from your body.'

Genesis 35:11

I AM

your mighty shield

✛

After these things the word of the
Lord came to Abram in a vision,
saying, 'Do not be afraid, Abram.
I am your shield, your exceedingly
great reward.'

Genesis 15:1

I AM

the Lion of the tribe of Judah

✛

But one of the elders said to me, 'Do
not weep. Behold, the Lion of the tribe
of Judah, the Root of David, has
prevailed to open the scroll and to
loose its seven seals.'

Revelation 5:5

322

I AM
the sword of the Spirit

✛

And take the helmet of salvation,

and the sword of the Spirit, which

is the word of God.

Ephesians 6:17

I AM

your high tower

✛

My lovingkindness and my fortress, my
high tower and my deliverer, my shield
and the One in whom I take refuge, who
subdues my people under me.

Psalm 144:2

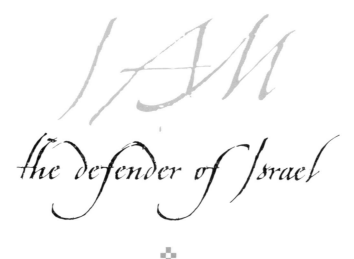

I AM

the defender of Israel

✛

Behold, He who keeps Israel shall
neither slumber nor sleep.

Psalm 121:4

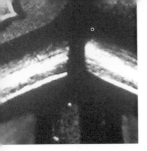

I AM

your fortress

✚

My lovingkindness and my fortress, my
high tower and my deliverer, my shield
and the One in whom I take refuge, who
subdues my people under me.

Psalm 144:2

I AM

omnipotent

✠

And I heard, as it were, the voice of a
great multitude, as the sound of many
waters and as the sound of mighty
thunderings, saying, 'Alleluia! For the
Lord God Omnipotent reigns!'

Revelation 19:6

I AM

the enemy of the enemies of Israel

✛

And the fear of God was on all the
kingdoms of those countries when
they heard that the Lord had fought
against the enemies of Israel.

2 Chronicles 20:29

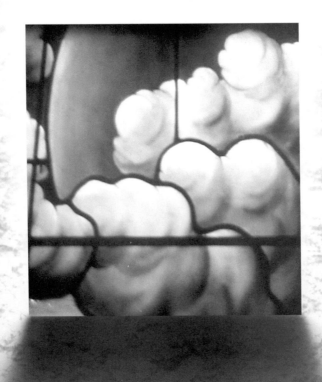

God is the same yesterday, today, and forever. He is the uncaused, eternal, self-existent One. He is the first and the last. He is the most powerful force in the universe. Before the mountains were brought forth, before the earth was formed, and even before time was created, God existed (Psalm 90:2). ✣ It is difficult to comprehend the eternal grandeur of God. The immensity of His dwelling place is impossible for time-focused, age-ravaged beings like us to comprehend. Everything we do is centered on time, and to understand eternity is often beyond our grasp. God existed before time was created and will exist long after earth has passed away. ✣ The time we spend on earth, and the decisions we make during our time here, will determine where we spend eternity. Small decisions have enormous, eternal consequences.

God of Eternity

I AM

I never change

✜

But He is unique, and who can
make Him change? And whatever
His soul desires, that He does.

Job 23:13

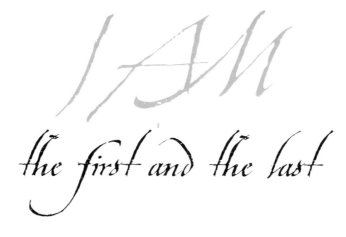

I AM

the first and the last

❖

Thus says the Lord, the King of Israel,
and his Redeemer, the Lord of hosts:
'I am the First and I am the Last;
besides Me there is no God.'

Isaiah 44:6

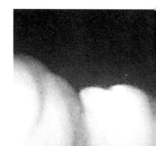

333

one

Hear, O Israel: The Lord our God,

the Lord is one!

Deuteronomy 6:4

I AM man's builder of faith through the ages

By faith he dwelt in the land of promise as in
a foreign country, dwelling in tents with Isaac
and Jacob, the heirs with him of the same
promise; for he waited for the city which has
foundations, whose builder and maker is God.

Hebrews 11:9-10

335

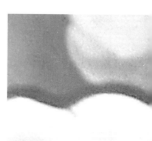

I AM

ruler of both the night and day

✤

Indeed, the darkness shall not hide
from You, but the night shines as
the day; the darkness and the light
are both alike to You.

Psalm 139:12

I AM

the uncaused, eternal, self-existent One

✦

Before the mountains were brought
forth, or ever You had formed the earth
and the world, even from everlasting to
everlasting, You are God.

Psalm 90:2

I AM

King forever and ever

✦

The Lord is King forever and ever; the
nations have perished out of His land.

Psalm 10:16

I AM

Spirit

✣

God is Spirit, and those who worship
Him must worship in spirit and truth.

John 4:24

I AM
the Alpha and the Omega

✤

I am the Alpha and the Omega,

the Beginning and the End,

the First and the Last.

Revelation 22:13

I AM

God whose eyes behold

✛

The Lord is in His holy temple,

the Lord's throne is in heaven;

His eyes behold, His eyelids

test the sons of men.

Psalm 11:4

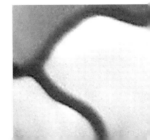

I AM

the same everyday

✛

Jesus Christ is the same yesterday,

today, and forever.

Hebrews 13:8

I AM

the Word of Life, called the Bible

✠

He was clothed with a robe dipped
in blood, and His name is called
The Word of God.

Revelation 19:13

343

I AM

the cornerstone

Therefore, to you who believe,

He is precious; but to those who

are disobedient, 'The stone which

the builders rejected has become

the chief cornerstone.'

1 Peter 2:7

344

I AM

the resurrection and the life

✤

Jesus said to her, 'I am the
resurrection and the life. He who
believes in Me, though he may die,
he shall live.'

John 11:25

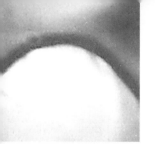

I AM

not of this world

✤

And He said to them, 'You are from
beneath; I am from above. You are of
this world; I am not of this world.'

John 8:23

I AM God who knows all My works through eternity

Known to God from eternity

are all His works.

Acts 15:18

347

I AM

omnipresent

✦

Where can I go from Your Spirit? Or
where can I flee from Your presence?

Psalm 139:7

I AM

the One who simultaneously sees beginning and end

✦

Declaring the end from the beginning,
and from ancient times things that are
not yet done, saying, 'My counsel shall
stand, and I will do all My pleasure.'

Isaiah 46:10

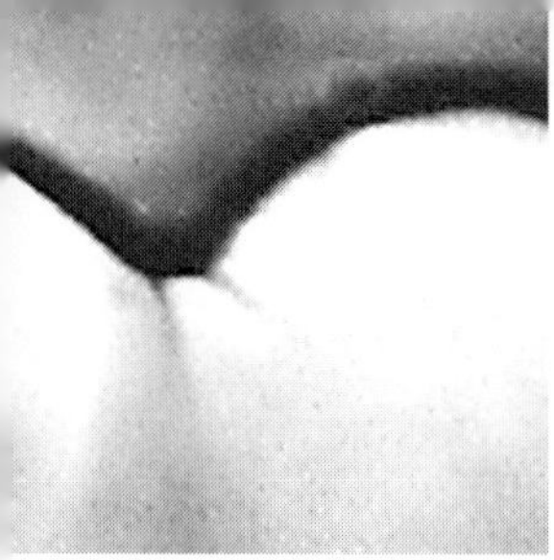

I AM

God, ready to perform My word

✣

Then the Lord said to me,
'You have seen well, for I am ready
to perform My word.'

Jeremiah 1:12

350

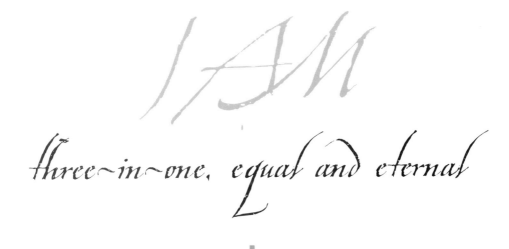

three~in~one, equal and eternal

✤

For there are three that bear witness in
heaven: the Father, the Word, and the
Holy Spirit; and these three are one.

1 John 5:7

I AM
before the day was

✠

Indeed before the day was,
I am He; and there is no one
who can deliver out of My hand;
I work, and who will reverse it?

Isaiah 43:13

I AM

all My names

✦

Speak to Aaron and his sons, that they
separate themselves from the holy
things of the children of Israel, and
that they do not profane My holy
name by what they dedicate to Me:
I am the Lord.

Leviticus 22:2

I AM

the self~sufficient, self~sustaining, self~creating One

✦

Then Moses said to God, 'Indeed, when I come to the children of Israel and say to them, "The God of your fathers has sent me to you," and they say to me, "What is His name?" what shall I say to them?' And God said to Moses, 'I AM WHO I AM.' And He said, 'Thus you shall say to the children of Israel, "I AM has sent me to you."'

Exodus 3:13-14

354

I AM

God, there is no other

✚

That they may know from the rising
of the sun to its setting that there
is none besides Me. I am the Lord,
and there is no other.

Isaiah 45:6

I AM

the Word, which was in the beginning

✦

In the beginning was the Word,

and the Word was with God,

and the Word was God.

John 1:1

I AM

the Rock of Ages on which you stand

✢

He only is my rock and my
salvation; He is my defense;
I shall not be moved.

Psalm 62:6

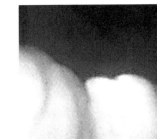

357

I AM

He who was, is, and is to come

✛

'I am the Alpha and the Omega,
the Beginning and the End,' says
the Lord, 'who is and who was and
who is to come, the Almighty.'

Revelation 1:8

I AM
Who I Am

✛

And God said to Moses,

'I AM WHO I AM.'

Exodus 3:14a

I AM

the everlasting God

✦

Then Abraham planted a
tamarisk tree in Beersheba,
and there called on the name of
the Lord, the Everlasting God.

Genesis 21:33

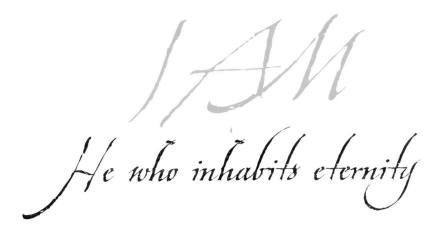

I AM

He who inhabits eternity

✦

For thus says the High and Lofty One who
inhabits eternity, whose name is Holy:
'I dwell in the high and holy place, with him
who has a contrite and humble spirit,
to revive the spirit of the humble, and to
revive the heart of the contrite ones.'

Isaiah 57:15

361

God is the Sovereign Ruler of the universe. He
rules over every creature in the heavens and on
the earth. He is the Lord of the cherubim and
seraphim and all heavenly creatures. He is the
King of kings, the Most High God, the Almighty,
and the Creator of life. ✦ As His creation,
we need God to shine brightly in and around
us, and to radiate from us. ✦ Think about
God's lordship over every creature. Ponder His
lordship in your life. Ask God to bring more
of His light into your life. Ask Him to
multiply the fruit of the Holy Spirit in your
spiritual walk. Ask Him to extend
His Kingdom blessing to every
area of your life. Ask Him
to release His creative nature
into every issue of
your life. Through His
divine power, inventions will be given, art will
be painted, music will be composed, poetry
will be written, and problems will be solved.

God of Every Creature

I AM the Lord, the fear of Me is the beginning of wisdom

The fear of the Lord is the beginning of wisdom; a good understanding have all those who do His commandments. His praise endures forever.

Psalm 111:10

I AM

the God of multiplication and reproduction

✛

Also God said to him: 'I am God
Almighty. Be fruitful and multiply; a
nation and a company of nations shall
proceed from you, and kings shall
come from your body.'

Genesis 35:11

I AM

Jehovah, that is My name

✛

That they may know that You, whose
name alone is the Lord, are the Most
High over all the earth.

Psalm 83:18

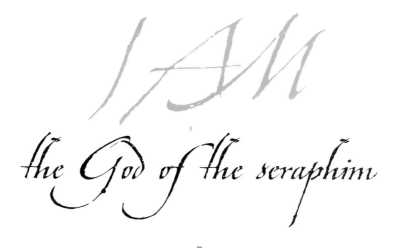

I AM

the God of the seraphim

❖

In the year that King Uzziah died, I saw the
Lord sitting on a throne, high and lifted up,
and the train of His robe filled the temple.
Above it stood seraphim; each one had six
wings: with two he covered his face, with two
he covered his feet, and with two he flew.

Isaiah 6:1-2

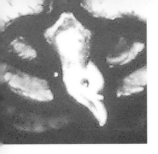

I AM

the God of all flesh

✣

Behold, I am the Lord, the God
of all flesh. Is there anything
too hard for Me?

Jeremiah 32:27

the vine

✜

I am the vine, you are the branches.
He who abides in Me, and I in him,
bears much fruit; for without Me
you can do nothing.

John 15:5

369

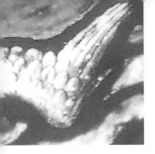

I AM

the artist that all artisans draw from

✤

And Bezalel and Aholiab, and every gifted
artisan in whom the Lord has put wisdom
and understanding, to know how to do all
manner of work for the service of the
sanctuary, shall do according to all that
the Lord has commanded.

Exodus 36:1

370

I AM

Adonai Eloheynu, there is none other

✣

That they may know from the rising
of the sun to its setting that there is
none besides Me. I am the Lord,
and there is no other.

Isaiah 45:6

371

I AM

the God of the cherubim

✣

And there I will meet with you, and I will
speak with you from above the mercy seat,
from between the two cherubim which are
on the ark of the Testimony, about
everything which I will give you in
commandment to the children of Israel.

Exodus 25:22

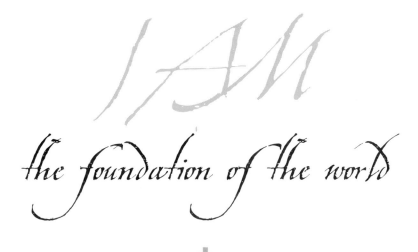

I AM

the foundation of the world

✣

The beast that you saw was, and is not, and will
ascend out of the bottomless pit and go to
perdition. And those who dwell on the earth will
marvel, whose names are not written in the Book
of Life from the foundation of the world, when
they see the beast that was, and is not, and yet is.

Revelation 17:8

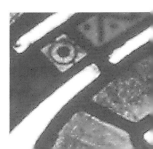

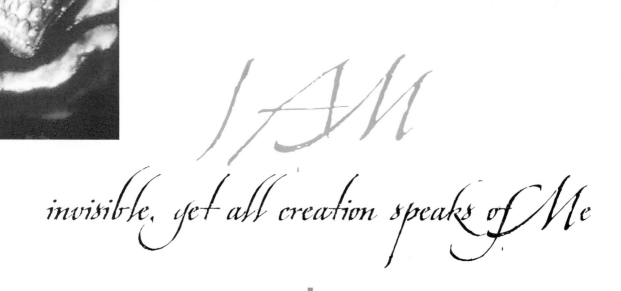

I AM
invisible, yet all creation speaks of Me

✛

For since the creation of the world His
invisible attributes are clearly seen, being
understood by the things that are made,
even His eternal power and Godhead, so
that they are without excuse. . .

Romans 1:20

I AM

God, I want you to understand and know Me

✛

But let him who glories glory in this,
that he understands and knows Me, that
I am the Lord, exercising lovingkindness,
judgment, and righteousness in the
earth. For in these I delight.

Jeremiah 9:24

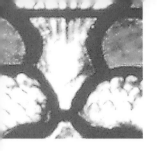

I AM

and you are My witnesses

❖

'I have declared and saved, I have
proclaimed, and there was no foreign god
among you; therefore you are My
witnesses,' says the Lord, 'that I am God.'

Isaiah 43:12

I AM

glorified in you

✛

And all Mine are Yours, and Yours are
Mine, and I am glorified in them.

John 17:10

I AM

*God who made you a sign
to the unbeliever*

Thus you will be a sign to them, and
they shall know that I am the Lord.

Ezekiel 24:27b

378

I AM

more than all structures of steel,
mortar, and clay

✜

'Heaven is My throne, and earth is
My footstool. What house will you
build for Me?' says the Lord. 'Or what
is the place of My rest?'

Acts 7:49

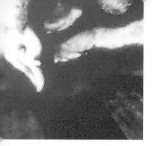

I AM

jealous over you

✛

. . .for you shall worship no other god,

for the Lord, whose name is Jealous,

is a jealous God.

Exodus 34:14

I AM

the exalted head over all

✣

Yours, O Lord, is the greatness, the
power and the glory, the victory and
the majesty; for all that is in heaven
and in earth is Yours; Yours is the
kingdom, O Lord, and You are
exalted as head over all.

1 Chronicles 29:11

381

I AM

God who is joined to the foreigner

✤

Do not let the son of the foreigner who
has joined himself to the Lord speak,
saying, 'The Lord has utterly separated
me from His people'; nor let the
eunuch say, 'Here I am, a dry tree.'

Isaiah 56:3

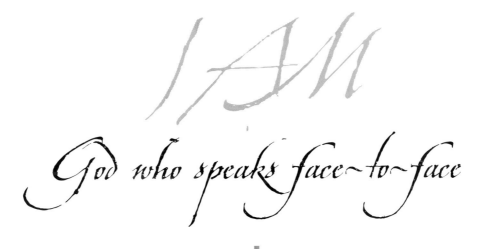

I AM

God who speaks face~to~face

✠

I speak with him face-to-face, even
plainly, and not in dark sayings; and
he sees the form of the Lord. Why then
were you not afraid to speak against
My servant Moses?

Numbers 12:8

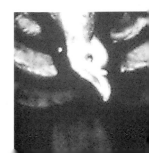

I AM

the sovereign ruler of all creation

✠

For 'He has put all things under
His feet.' But when He says
'all things are put under Him,' it is
evident that He who put all things
under Him is excepted.

1 Corinthians 15:27

I AM

your next breath

✛

You hide Your face, they are troubled;

You take away their breath, they die

and return to their dust.

Psalm 104:29

I AM

the light of the world

✤

Then Jesus spoke to them again,

saying, 'I am the light of the world. He

who follows Me shall not walk in

darkness, but have the light of life.'

John 8:12

I AM

God and all that is in Heaven and in earth is Mine

✦

Yours, O Lord, is the greatness, the power
and the glory, the victory and the majesty;
for all that is in heaven and in earth is
Yours; Yours is the kingdom, O Lord, and
You are exalted as head over all.

1 Chronicles 29:11

I AM

Immanuel, God dwelling among men

✠

Behold, the virgin shall be with child,

and bear a Son, and they shall call

His name Immanuel, which is

translated, God with us.

Matthew 1:23

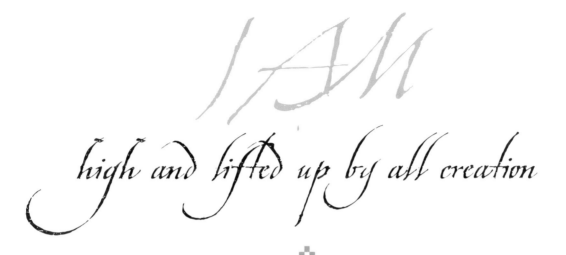

I AM

high and lifted up by all creation

✤

In the year that King Uzziah died,
I saw the Lord sitting on a throne,
high and lifted up, and the train of
His robe filled the temple.

Isaiah 6:1

389

I AM
the outpoured Spirit on all flesh

✠

And it shall come to pass in the last
days, says God, that I will pour out of
My Spirit on all flesh; your sons and
your daughters shall prophesy, your
young men shall see visions, your old
men shall dream dreams.

Acts 2:17

I AM

He who rejoices with those who rejoice

✜

Rejoice with those who rejoice, and
weep with those who weep.

Romans 12:15

I AM

the only creator of all that exists

✤

I have made the earth, and created
man on it. I – My hands – stretched
out the heavens, and all their host I
have commanded.

Isaiah 45:12

I AM

Savior of both the Gentiles and the Jews

For there is no distinction between Jew
and Greek, for the same Lord over all
is rich to all who call upon Him.
For 'whoever calls on the name of
the Lord shall be saved.'

Romans 10:12-13

I AM
He before whom every knee will bow

✛

For it is written: 'As I live, says the
Lord, every knee shall bow to Me, and
every tongue shall confess to God.'

Romans 14:11